T0067165

OTHER PUBLICATIONS

When Do The Tears Stop?
First published – Author House 2010
Second edition – Kingprint 2014
ISBN: 978-1-4520-6403-1

Spirit Speaks
Balboa Press – 2016
ISBN: 978-1-5034-0390-3(sc)
ISBN: 978-1-5043-0389-7(e)

Walking with Spirit
First Published – iUniverse 2012

Poetry Books:

Language Of Love   ISBN: 978-1-4716-1632-7
Love Potion   ISBN: 0-9587427-0-7
Intermesh   (Out of print)
Odyssey   (Out of print)

www.joybrisbane.com

Spirit Alliance

The Connection Between
Mind, Heart, and Soul

Joy Brisbane

BALBOA.
PRESS

A DIVISION OF HAY HOUSE

Balboa Press books may be ordered through booksellers or by contacting:

Balboa Press
A Division of Hay House
1663 Liberty Drive
Bloomington, IN 47403
www.balboapress.com.au
1 (877) 407-4847

Because of the dynamic nature of the Internet, any web addresses or links contained in this book may have changed since publication and may no longer be valid. The views expressed in this work are solely those of the author and do not necessarily reflect the views of the publisher, and the publisher hereby disclaims any responsibility for them.

The author of this book does not dispense medical advice or prescribe the use of any technique as a form of treatment for physical, emotional, or medical problems without the advice of a physician, either directly or indirectly. The intent of the author is only to offer information of a general nature to help you in your quest for emotional and spiritual well-being. In the event you use any of the information in this book for yourself, which is your constitutional right, the author and the publisher assume no responsibility for your actions.

Any people depicted in stock imagery provided by Thinkstock are models, and such images are being used for illustrative purposes only.
Certain stock imagery © Thinkstock.

Print information available on the last page.

ISBN: 978-1-5043-1045-1 (sc)
ISBN: 978-1-5043-1046-8 (e)

Balboa Press rev. date: 09/20/2017

Thank You

To my dear friend and editor
Dallas Kinnear
For the many hours you have dedicated to this book,
For the way you have challenged me,
For your belief in me
And
For your love.

Also

I dedicate this book to Mary Salopek and Lynne Saunders.
Thank you for your wisdom, patience and love.
Thank you for helping me to heal.
Without you this book could not have been written.

CONTENTS

INTRODUCTION

I have known since the age of seven I have had an alliance with the realm of spirit. My abilities as a psychic medium continued to develop through my years at school, nursing training, and my training in counselling. My alliance with my spirit guides has helped me through many challenging times.

My battle with grief after the death of my second husband in 2002, and my experiences of making contact with him through the spirit world, brought me to the realisation that my gifts and training could combine to help other people move through their grief. I began in a quiet way to reach out to other people, sharing my gifts as a medium and my training as a counsellor to help others reclaim happiness in their lives. My clientele quickly increased.

I have researched and studied the realm of spirit extensively, seeking to understand my gifts as a psychic medium. I have also had two near-death experiences, the result of anaphylactic reactions after insect bites. During my out of body experiences, I caught a glimpse of the beauty, the splendour of the realm of spirit, validating my research and the visions I had been receiving since a child.

Through the written word, I hope to touch the lives of others and help them to find the joy and peace I have found in my own life.

Joy

1   *Walking With Spirit*

I WAS BROUGHT UP on a farm in the Western District of Victoria, Australia. It was there I first became aware of the importance Mother Nature plays in our existence. It was also there I first became aware of my gift as a psychic medium. But at that time, sadly, psychic ability was treated with great suspicion, condemned as being the workings of dark forces, or totally disbelieved. For my parents, it was a mixture of disbelief and fear of the darkness.

I quickly learned not to speak of the beautiful beings I was seeing. They popped in on a daily basis to say hello, my lovely ones, my guides, keeping the communication between us intact. I, at that stage, had no understanding why they were with me; no understanding that these beings of light were assigned to this less than perfect individual to help me on my life's journey. For me, they were just my mates with whom I held important conversations (out of earshot of my mother).

As the teen years filled my head with ideas of romance, how to overcome pimples, and how to get out of study but still pass school exams, the unseen ones gracefully and quietly waited for me to grow up and evolve into womanhood.

At seventeen, I began training to become a nurse. Throughout my years as a nurse, I began to realise there was a lot more to my guides' presence in my life than just good mates. It was not only a time of training in becoming a healer; it was also a time of discovery in psychic phenomena. I had many strange experiences during that time.

Then I married and had two children. My first marriage was eight years of struggle; it ended in divorce. But the one thing my husband and I had in common was the ability to see UFOs and to experience the paranormal. It was the first time I had been able to speak openly of some of the experiences I was having. Apart from the precious gift of two children, I now know it was a time of validation for me, something for me to hold on to as the years ahead brought many challenges. During this time, I trained as a Lifeline counsellor, Australia's national phone counselling service.

Lifeline was begun to help those in need of instant counselling, such as people who were suicidal. Later it expanded to include people isolated by distance, such as in the outback parts of Australia, for those who are struggling financially, and for those with issues that arise in the middle of the night when all other help organizations are closed.

My second marriage was a happy one, but my husband, Jeff, did not believe in my gift as a psychic medium or share my beliefs about the afterlife. His objections were so strong that I could not talk to him about my experiences. We lived on seven acres of isolated land, surrounded by thousands of acres of eucalyptus forest. A gentle stream ran through our property just fifty metres from our house. It was here I first discovered my ability to see the energy of wildlife. Communication with birds and animals led to a powerful period of awakening and growth in my abilities. But it was in some ways a lonely journey; there was no one I could fully trust to share my insights and experiences.

When Jeff died in 2002, I had no one left to appease or answer to. I decided the time had come for me to take the risk and allow the gifts with which I was born to fully develop. I came out of the proverbial closet and fully stepped into my truth. It was a scary journey, requiring a lot of strength and courage (at a time when grief filled my heart), but through it all my lovely ones in spirit held me in their love. Friends turned away from me. But in return I gained a sense of peace and stillness that, at long last, I could be truly *me*! Many beautiful friends have since replaced the ones who no longer have contact with me.

Since that time, I have completed many courses that allow me to work with people, helping them to heal, to find direction in life, to discover their own beautiful selves, and to awaken them to the help they have from the realm of spirit through their guides and loved ones who have died. It is wonderfully rewarding work, and there have been many occasions when I have felt deeply humbled to be part of the intimate world of my fellow human beings. I am now doing what I came here to do, and I will not leave until my work has been completed.

Sometimes it takes strength and courage to stand in our truth and to walk our own path. Others may not understand. Life can deal us challenges that are difficult. But always, when we are true to ourselves there comes a sense of peace and stillness. We will find that strength and courage to do what we know is right for us to do, and then we realise that life is a marvellous journey!

2   *Religion Or Spirituality?*

IS THERE A DIFFERENCE between religion and spirituality? And if so, what is that difference?

For me, there is no right or wrong way to deal with these questions. No doubt there will be those who will disagree with me, and they have the right to do so. I am not concerned with agreement or disagreement; my only concern is for individuals to find the path that is right for them. What I share with you are my own personal beliefs. All I ask is for you to have an open mind and to explore what feels right for you.

I perceive the difference between religion and spirituality to be this:

Religion is a coming together of a group of people with the same beliefs to worship the same deity, such as Christians, Buddhists, Muslims, followers of the Hindu gods or goddess, or any other form of organised worship. Usually there are guidelines for people to follow, and they adhere to sacred ceremonies. Within most religions there is a hierarchy of the learned ones, the teachers or the leaders, down to the common worshipper.

Spirituality, on the other hand, is an inner journey with self; with my heart and soul and their connection to that divine energy I call Great Spirit. It is a deeply personal, loving relationship between the realm of spirit and self. I prefer Great Spirit to God. For me the words "Great Spirit" remove the religious connotations; they therefore encompass all people, all of life upon this planet, and, indeed, of all the cosmos. I see spiritual growth as the bringing together of heart, mind, and soul, an awakening to the beauty within us and around us, the evolution into our inner divine love for self and love for all that is.

This does not mean that the two do not go hand in hand. They can and do for a great number of people. One of the most devoutly religious and deeply spiritual people I have known was my mother. My dad was a wonderful man, but he was a born-again Christian, and at times it was difficult for me to see the spirituality in amongst the religion. The difference between the two; my dad lived his Christianity through fear of judgement beyond death; my mother lived her Christianity through love. My father pushed religion onto his children; my mother showed her spirituality by simply being the quiet, gentle, and loving person she was. Poor Dad, if he only knew it, Mum had a far deeper and more sustaining effect on my spiritual development than he could ever have. But I bless him for it. Without realising what he was doing, he gave me a clear understanding of the difference between religion and spirituality.

Like me, more and more people these days are choosing to not belong to any organization that is of a religious nature. Instead, we are finding our own deep and personal inner experience with that amazing divine essence I call Great Spirit. There are many paths to the top of the same mountain. None of them are right or wrong, they just simply *are*!

I don't believe that a Great Spirit, capable of creating an entire cosmos, would be all that concerned as to how I, one individual, on this tiny planet, perceives my religious or spiritual experience. And I don't think that such a magnificent spirit would be all that pleased with the inhabitants of Earth using religion as an excuse to create wars. We were given a thing called free will, and therefore we can choose what is right for us as we allow ourselves to explore our spiritual and religious beliefs.

The more I work as a medium, connecting in to the realm of spirit, the more I realise how little I know. The realm of spirit is way beyond my human ability to fully comprehend how it works and what it looks like. I get glimpses into colours so amazingly beautiful there is no way to describe them. I get to hear faint strands of music more sublime than anything created by the greatest composers throughout the centuries. I get to see fabulous beings of love and light that are so magnificent I am pulled into absolute humility and tears of joyfulness. All the while, I know I am only seeing or hearing a tiny drop in an immense cosmic ocean of love. It is an incredibly privileged place to be, and yet we are all connected to that love, that beauty, that powerful energy called spirit.

Religion is about worshipping that divine energy through rites and established guidelines of behaviour. Spirituality is a personal and inner journey that directly connects us to that energy and brings us into a realisation that we are one with and a part of Great Spirit, and Great Spirit is one with and a part of us.

3 *What Is Psychic Ability?*

I AM OFTEN ASKED how my psychic ability works; people wonder how this "stuff" happens.

Every single person on this planet has psychic ability. We are born with it, and we all use it every day of our life without being aware that we do. Many highly qualified doctors are now studying psychic ability in scientific ways including Dr Melvin Morse, author of *Parting Visions* ; Dr Brian Weiss, author of *Many Lives, Many Masters* and *Messages From The Masters*; and Dr Michael Newton, author of *Journey Of Souls* and *Destiny Of Souls*.

These are just three people who have been intrigued enough to delve deeper. They are concluding what psychic people have known for centuries; that we do indeed have psychic abilities, have near-death experiences, can recall past lives, can chat with beings in spirit, and have dreams that hold powerful messages for our lives.

There is a difference between psychic abilities and the abilities of a medium.

Psychic abilities are tools, no different to the screwdriver in the carpenter's hand, to be used for the betterment of ourselves and those with whom we come into contact. They are aligned to our senses:

- Sight (clairvoyance)
- Smell
- Taste
- Hearing (clairaudience)
- Feeling (clairsentience) and
- Intuition (clair cognisance)

A medium is someone who can slide into other realms and communicate with those who have died, people from other planets, the realm of fairies, the realm of the masters, and the realm of angels. As a medium, the two strongest psychic gifts are clairvoyance and clairaudience, although the other psychic senses are handy in making the connection stronger and clearer.

I have known since I was a child that I had the ability to talk to beings from other realms. However, when I decided to do this work as a medium, the old doubts and fears arose to challenge my belief in self and in the lovely ones I have around me, my guides. It was part of my learning process to realise those of us who work with our psychic abilities are human. At all times, we need to remain grounded and sensible in this work, trusting in what comes through, learning to get our ego out of the way and let spirit work through us.

I am going to share a session I had with a couple who came to see me, but to allow them their privacy, I have changed their names to Bob and Betty. Their story is not uncommon. They came to see me in the earlier days when I finally came out of hiding and stepped into doing this work. I will never forget this session. It was not only about them, it was as though my guides were showing me the importance of using my gifts to help others and to trust in what comes through.

Here is their story:

Betty rang me to make an appointment to speak with her mother, who had died. For the week prior to her arrival, a rather troubled spirit of a man had been bugging me. I knew his life had not been a healthy one. I kept getting glimpses of things he had done that were not pleasant to see.

Betty arrived, accompanied by Bob, her husband. As he walked in the door, arms folded, he said, "I have come to just let you know that I think this is all bullshit!" My anger immediately bubbled to the surface. I said, "Well this is not actually about you, and I am not concerned with what you think. If you intend to stay, then you will sit down and shut up. This is for your wife and her mother, and it matters not that you don't believe in it. Everyone has the right to believe what they damn well like!" I looked quickly at his wife and saw her distress. I immediately felt remorse for having put her in that position, and I felt very unprofessional.

To try and calm the whole atmosphere down, I then apologized for my anger, asked them to be seated, and made them a cup of tea. (Don't underestimate the effects of the good old "cuppa." The mums and grans of old knew something about giving troubled people a cuppa at the kitchen table.) As I was making the tea, the man in spirit stood beside me, saying, "Tell him; tell him." Then I knew this man was Bob's father! I also knew that I was wrong; this was about Bob as well as Betty. It was actually about them as a couple. The knowledge that their marriage was in trouble because of Bob's anger toward his father was made very clear to me. Our loved ones on the other side are clever little bunnies; Betty's mum and Bob's dad had got together to try and work a miracle and save their children's marriage.

When I sat down, I looked at Bob and said, "I am ok with you not believing. You are as entitled to not believe as I am to believe. There is no right or wrong here, just experience. However, I have had a man in spirit with me all week, and I know it is your dad, and he has a hell of a lot to say to you." With that, it was like his father showed me a film of his life.

9

Bob's dad had been an alcoholic, wasted all of their money on gambling and beer, belted Bob's mother from time to time, had a fight with two men outside the pub where he drank (which he showed me in great detail), and had interfered sexually with Bob's two sisters. He then showed me the house where he used to live (again in great detail) and the rubbish that piled up in the back yard. The clarity with which it all came through was awesome. And then Bob's dad said, "Tell him his anger at me is sending him down the same path I went down, and it will destroy his marriage if he doesn't do something about it. Tell him I know he has not been sexually active with Betty for the past five years because his anger at me is stopping him from being a loving husband. Tell him I am so sorry and I seek his forgiveness."

This session changed the lives of these two people. Two days later, Betty rang me to say how "blown away" Bob had been by the experience. He sent her flowers to her place of work the next day, with a card that said, "Please try and get off work early today. I have arranged for the kids to be cared for by a friend overnight. I am taking you out for dinner. I love you." They had little sleep during that night as they talked through all of their issues. It was a night of intimate and sensual reunion, the reawakening of their love.

Betty did get to talk with her mother, who also relayed back to them a whole heap of stuff I could not have possibly known about. Mum and Dad on the other side did a pretty good job at bringing about healing for their children.

What was my role in all of this? Simply to show up and say yes to willingly facilitate the connection! More importantly, my role was to *trust*…trust Bob's dad, trust Betty's mum, trust my guides, and trust that all was as it was meant to be. Does this stuff work? Yes! How does it work? One day, perhaps the scientists can tell us.

4 *Cellular Memory*

THE TERM "CELLULAR MEMORY" has been around for quite some time. The definition seems simple enough: the storage, at a physical level, in muscle, bone, organs and tissue, of events both painful and pleasurable of our past and present lives.

But how do these memories become stored in our physical bodies? One tends to think of memory as an activity of the brain, and that in itself is an amazing occurrence. How does our brain hold in its grey matter not only the memory of this lifetime but also of past lives?

There is no doubt of the existence of cellular memory. Medical science proves such memory does exist. Patients who have received transplant organs, particularly those of the heart, have been known to suddenly desire certain foods and drinks that they were once never interested in or to do activities they have never done before. On examination, it is found that those interests were a strong part of the donor's lifestyle. And of course there are many stories told of phantom pain in limbs that have been removed. How does one feel pain where a limb no longer exists?

We are becoming more open and aware of how past lives can affect our present life at a mental and emotional level, but are we also aware of how past lives (and past events of our present life) are affecting us physically through cellular memory?

How does my physical body, when it is constantly renewing itself, retain a memory not only of this life but also past lives? Every seven years, my body has gone through a complete renewal process. Not a single cell that is in my body right now, in this moment in time, will be present in seven years. My belief is that it is not my body as such that has the memory, but my soul!

Our physical forms are the vehicles in which the soul resides until death brings a separation of soul from its host, the body. At that time, the soul returns home to its soul family. Dr Michael Newton in his book *Journey of Souls* gives a wonderful account of our soul families and how they are formed. Once the soul has returned, at some point it will contemplate another reincarnation in order to continue to learn and grow into its rightful magnificence.

When we first enter our host body as a little babe within the womb, our soul brings with it the memories needed for its continued growth in this particular incarnation. In its present life, it continues to build upon its memory bank. As we enter the body, we infuse into the heavy vibrational energy of physical matter our lighter vibrational energy of the soul. The two vibrations become one: soul and body. As the two energies merge, our physical self absorbs the memory of the soul. In doing so, it also absorbs the memory of past lives and continues to absorb the memories of our present life.

Hence it matters not that my body renews itself every seven years. The process of cellular memory is an ongoing one as the memory of the soul is continuously being integrated or infused into the heavier vibration of my physical matter.

The implications of how cellular memory works is enormous and, I believe, directly relates to our physical health. How many present day illnesses, such as arthritis, alcoholism, cancer and asthma, actually have their foundation in cellular memory? We are learning to treat physical illnesses as part of a mental or emotional journey. Perhaps we also need to put into the equation the healing of cellular memory. We are, after all, four parts: thought, emotion, body and soul/spirit. When helping any singular one of these to heal, I believe we need to look at the other three and see what part they are playing in the disease.

For example: can depression actually have its roots, its foundation, in the cellular memory of a past life? When I think back through the centuries to the continuous wars this planet has known, the poverty and starvation, how much of the history of this cellular memory is actually causing the depression we are now seeing?

I don't believe that it is always necessary to remember what the past lives were about. I believe one can deal with cellular memory without knowing the journey behind it. In simply being aware that our cellular memory does play a major part in our journey of healing, we can then clear that memory through meditation; energy healing, such as Reiki or Theta; hypnosis (as Dr Brian Weiss does); or any number of ways that suits the individual. If the best way to clear the cellular memory is through past-life recall, so be it; remember, this is not a game. It is important, when we seek out this form of healing, to make sure we have a good practitioner who knows how to integrate what is revealed with what is happening for us in this lifetime.

5   *The Healing Power Of Humour*

A FEW YEARS AGO, I connected with a man I will simply call Grandpa. Grandpa came through for his grandson, who had come to see me. One of the things that impressed me with this spirit was the great expanse of his energy and his wonderful sense of humour.

Grandpa taught me that humour is a wonderful aid in helping us to heal. It helps to keep us from going down into our negative, ego-based feelings, and in doing so, it fast tracks the healing process. For those who are terminally ill, it helps to prepare them for their journey into a new life, to heal at a soul level.

Grandpa had died of a rare bone disease that had been extremely debilitating and very painful. The disease was diagnosed at a time when the strength of youth and the accumulation of wisdom from life's experiences were beginning to come together, in that wonderful period of forty to fifty years of age.

When I see and feel such bigness of energy, it usually means I am in the presence of a highly evolved soul. There was a radiant joy emanating from him. He evoked in me an excitement and the desire to laugh. I knew I was in the presence of someone very special. There was warmth, and his humour was gentle and playful.

Humour helped Grandpa from sinking into the depths of depression. He used humour to help him get through the long days. The seemingly endless nights became a time to explore his thoughts and feelings about self and life in general. It was a time of contemplation and prayer as he prepared himself for his homeward journey.

Grandpa not only used humour to keep himself from sinking into despair, he also used it to help ease the discomfort of friends when they visited him. Humour helped the members of his family as they began to feel the crippling grief of knowing that his time with them was drawing to a close. I sensed that there were times when those closest to him became irritated with his humour, believing that he was avoiding the truth with his apparently flippant comments. But Grandpa knew fully what was before him, and humour helped him to cope, helped him to help those he most loved. But perhaps more importantly, humour helped him to heal at a soul/spirit level, allowing him to accept the journey that lay in front of him.

Grandpa wanted to have a chat with his grandson, but he also saw the chance to bring a message to people struggling with life-threatening illnesses. Part of that message was to develop a mindfulness of our moods and practice humour when the challenges of life are likely to send us into anxiety and despair.

We have a choice to allow ourselves to be swallowed by the darkness or to seek out the light. Humour can flick the switch that fills a dark room with light. It is the match that lights the candle. Within an instant, humour can turn a dull and boring party into a time of laughter and fun. And so it can also change a despairing heart and mind.

When my husband died suddenly in 2002, one of the things that helped me to move through those first painful months was humour. It was a balm to my aching heart and a relief to my troubled mind.

It is why comedians are so important in our entertainment world. They help us to put our troubles aside for a time. They fill us with the beauty and energy of laughter. Without knowing it, they are helping us to heal. Watching funny films is a time of escape from the troubles of life, a rest for our weary minds, and respite for our painful hearts.

I believe our wonderful guides have great amounts of humour. Sometimes we take our spiritual journey so seriously, we miss out on the joyfulness of our experiences. I am constantly getting the message from my lovely guides, "Lighten up! Why are you so serious? Don't you realise this is meant to be a joyful, happy journey?"

We draw to ourselves the negative aspects of life when we are constantly living with tension. When we let go of tension and bring in laughter, our life flows more smoothly and our risk of disease diminishes. Two people who know the power of laughter and joyfulness are Patch Adams and Dr Robert Holden, author of *Happiness Now* and *Be Happy*.

Patch Adams is that amazing doctor from the United States of America who has created clowns to go into hospitals all over this planet. Patch knows the benefit, the healing quality of fun and laughter. (Watch the DVD called PATCH of his true life story). A major component of the healing process in his clinic is humour, and his studies are proving that with the use of humour, his clients are healing much faster than the patients suffering from the same illnesses elsewhere.

Humour could not heal Grandpa's body, but it made his painful journey (and the journey of his loved ones) much easier to bear. There was nothing that could have prevented Grandpa from passing through the curtain of death, but whilst his body was dying, his mind, heart, and soul were healing through his wonderful attitude and his delightful gift of humour.

Remember: the greatest lesson we are all here on this planet to learn is how to live with a joyful heart, a relaxed and peaceful mind, and a radiant soul. Grandpa not only had the chance to chat with his grandson, he helped me to look at life in a different way. I hope his message continues on, touching your life as he has touched mine.

MEDITATION

Put on some soft and gentle music; the kind of music that will help you move deeper into a meditative space. Use instrumental music so you do not become distracted by the words. Turn off your phones and make sure you will not be interrupted as you do this meditation. If it is difficult to find time in your home environment for you to do this meditation, then drive to a park and sit in your car and meditate in peace and quiet, or sit by the ocean. A church or a temple are also places where you can meditate undisturbed.

Take a few deep breaths until you begin to feel your whole body coming into a state of deep relaxation. Let go of the thoughts about what needs to be done. Allow this time to be just for you. If you are a person who has difficulty with creating visions in your mind, then just use your ability to sense what is happening.

Once you are in a relaxed state of mind and body, visualise yourself in a park where there are swings and things for children to enjoy a time of playfulness. Sit on the grass or on a bench seat. The sun is gently shining; its warmth soaks your body in a way that makes you feel nurtured. As you watch the children playing, you become aware of another being, a spirit, dancing around the children, laughing and playful. The children, preoccupied with their playfulness, are unaware of the presence of this beautiful being amongst them. This being is dressed in a brightly coloured rainbow garment that swirls. There is such a sense of joyfulness here in this park, and yet there is also peace and gentleness.

This beautiful spirit being becomes aware of your presence and quietly glides over to where you are and sits beside you. This spirit being takes your hand and begins to speak to you.

"What are your thoughts as you watch the children at play?" the spirit being asks. "Do you wish you could play like them again? How do you feel as you sit here quietly watching? Would you like to join us? See how carefree they are. Each one of these children has problems, just like you. Their parents are separating, or they are being bullied at school, or they feel inadequate because the others appear to be so smart. These children have problems just as you do, and yet they are able to let go of those problems as they indulge in the joyfulness of playtime. I am your guide assigned to help you overcome your negative thoughts and feelings and to find the joy in your life. All tough experiences have powerful lessons for you to learn, but even in the toughest experience you can still find time to laugh and be playful. Laughter and playfulness will help you to swing through the tough times and help you to dance into healing the pain in your mind and heart. Come with me, come and join the children; allow yourself to be a child for a little while, to feel the freedom of being playful. Come and dance with me."

Take this being's hand, stand up, and allow yourself to move into the dance with uninhibited sensual and joyful movements. Feel the freedom that comes with the dance and allow yourself to be playful, to laugh, and to have fun with your new guide. With the playfulness comes a deep sense of peace, of release from your problems, and a renewing of your energy.

Your guide leads you to a seesaw, and you both move up and down on the seesaw, feeling the freedom of movement as you rise into the air and then become grounded again. You guide brings you to a level place with the seesaw. As you sit there looking at each other, your guide says, "See what it is like when you become unbalanced; one moment you are up in the air and the next moment you have hit the ground. Humour balances out the tension and burdens of your life."

Next you are led to a merry-go-round. The music plays as you ride your horse, round and round. Your guide calls to you, "Is this how your life feels, as though you are going round and round in circles getting nowhere? In truth your journey with your soul is more than a circle, it is a spiral forever winding upwards. Even though you may feel you are only going around in circles, each turn takes you to another level, forever upwards. Listen to the music of your heart and enjoy the ride."

Your guide continues to speak. "Every aspect of this playground is a metaphor for your life. When you feel you are on the slide and you have hit the bottom, turn around and climb back up again. Now come, dance with me and let the dance carry you into the joyfulness of life."

Spend a little time with your guide. Enjoy the joyfulness, the freedom of the dance. When you are ready, take a deep breath and let it out slowly. Wiggle your toes and fingers. Come back gently into the room. Become aware of the sounds of the outer world. Again, when you are ready, open your eyes.

Every time your troubles seem to overwhelm you, go back into this meditation and ask your guide for help. Give your guide a name, a fun name that will help you to seek out and communicate with this guide again and again throughout your life. Trust that this guide is present in your life, and seek to develop a deep and personal relationship with this beautiful being.

As I have discovered, help is just a whisper away!

6   *The Healing Power Of Colour*

WHEN I FIRST SAW Grandpa, he presented himself in a wheel chair so I could understand how his illness had affected him. His energy field was blotchy; mostly cloudy-grey with touches of dark red and vibrant yellow. There were three dark patches, indicating holes in his energy field, places where the energy had completely disappeared; the back of his head, his upper back, and one at his lower back and hips (indicating spinal damage and hip joint damage). The dark red felt to me like he was trying to remain grounded but doing so in the midst of a lot of pain. The bright yellow (in complete contrast to the rest of his energy field) indicated his ability to remain a powerful being in the midst of trauma, his use of humour and the ability to pull himself out of depression.

Once I had seen what Grandpa had been through, he then presented himself as he was in the present moment: standing erect, youthful, handsome, and full of vitality. His energy field was mainly a wonderful golden shimmering light with flashes of a rich, deep pink and a bright, deep royal blue. These colours told me that his soul had completely healed from the effects of his illness. The golden shimmering light was who he truly was, the essence of his being. The deep pink indicated to me divine love, his love for his fellow souls, and the deep, bright royal blue his ability to help others to heal and to connect with them, bringing messages to help them on their life's journey. This was a soul who had evolved through trials and pain to stand magnificently in his god-like essence.

Colour plays an important roll in our lives. Colours have many interpretations; these explanations are as individual as we are. There is no right or wrong to colour interpretation. Bright red for one person may mean anger; for another vitality, passion, and sensuality; and for another the need to be grounded and to deal with insecurities. Pale blue for one person may mean weak and insipid, for another loving and gentle, and for others it may mean creativity.

What may be exquisite for one person may be boring for another. This was brought home to me by a man with whom I was interested in forming a relationship. One evening, when I knew he was coming to see me, I went to a lot of trouble to make sure I looked pretty and well-groomed. I wore my favourite colour, purple, because I always felt good, sensual, and very much a woman whenever I wore purple. As I opened the door to him, he said, "Oh God, no, not another purple woman!" (Well that was the end of him!) Weeks later, I went to the funeral of a dear friend and wore the same garments. Another male friend of mine came up to me and whispered in my ear, "You know, I always like you in that colour. It suits you!" Ah, such a balm to the ego!

We all have our individual interpretation and response to colours. When someone is interpreting colour for us, we need to see how we feel about their interpretation. It is important not to blindly follow what someone else says. I know what feels right for me, but my interpretation of colour may not be the same as yours.

Let's have a look at the two elements of colours, firstly as a mirror for who we are and then at their healing qualities.

THE MIRROR:

Wearing purple when my male visitor came to call was my way to validate who I am. It was a reminder that I am a strong, sensual, deeply spiritual, and loving woman. At a subconscious level, I had hoped that by wearing purple he would see me for who I truly am. His reaction should have been my first warning that perhaps this relationship had nowhere to go! To him, purple represented an ungrounded, airy-fairy spiritual woman. To me, purple is a sensual and sexy colour. My dress acted as a mirror for both of us.

We often tell someone, "You know, that colour looks really good on you!" or "That person really should not wear that colour!" Sure, their skin type, eye colour, and hair play a part in it, but I believe it is more than those physical features; I believe it is as much about what colours are showing in our energy field and about our soul's essence.

Do I dress in certain colours because I am making a statement about who I am? Or do I dress in certain colours because that is who I want to be? I personally think both are true; there is no defining line between the two.

When we wear colours that don't suit us (that in some way clash with our skin type and personality), it may be a sign that we are out of touch with our deeper essence, our soul essence.

From time to time, look in your wardrobe and assess the colours you have in there. Ask yourself, "Why do I wear a lot of that particular colour?" Is it because that is who I perceive myself to be? Or is it because I am lacking in self-esteem and that colour hides me? Colours can help to lift our spirits and help us become the person we really want to be, or they can act as a screen, closing us off from the world.

THE HEALING QUALITIES

Individual colours have individual healing qualities. Colour deeply affects our minds and emotions.

Hospitals have long since known that their walls, floors, and bedding need to be soft colours: pale pinks, blues, greens, off white, beige…. because harsh and bright colours are uncomfortable for people when they are feeling ill. Patients need soft and nurturing colours that are gentle in their impact when they are under stress because of their illness. Conversely, children's playgrounds often have bright and bold colours that draw the young ones to them with their seductive inference of fun and vitality. Just take a look at the McDonalds play areas. What does their playground say to the young ones? "Hey, kids, look at what we have got for you, a lovely bright play area where you can have fun…. after you have had your food and while mum and dad are eating!"

Experiment

Close your eyes and image yourself in a green forest, sitting beneath a tree with its green canopy shading you from the hot midday sun. How does it make you feel to be in all that greenness? Imagine yourself walking beside the blue ocean on a gentle summer's day. Look out to sea. How does the blue-green of the ocean make you feel? Now image yourself riding a camel through a treeless desert with yellow sand and brown rocks. How does that make you feel? And now visualize yourself watching a vibrant sunset. Even in our imagination these colours can change our moods. To try and gain some perspective of how those colours affected you, now visualize each of the above landscapes being all black and white. Somehow, a black-and-white forest or sunset just doesn't do it for me! The missing element is the healing factor of green in the forest and red, yellow, pink, purple, and blue of the sunset.

When I first saw the colours (or lack of them) in Grandpa's energy field, I immediately felt compassion for the pain he had experienced. But when I saw how his energy field looked after his healing, I had an immediate response of joyfulness. It brought tears running down my face to see the incredible change he had experienced in his healing at a soul level.

We don't have to wait until we are dead and pass over to our soul's home to begin that healing process. It can begin now, and we can know *now* the joyfulness of stepping into the vibrant colours we are meant to be at a soul level.

I have been trained in the art of Theta Energy healings. Like Reiki, Theta healings are a hands-on form of healing where the practitioner moves into a hypnotic state to bring through the powerful healing energies from highly evolved beings in the realm of spirit. Whilst working with a client, I am usually told (by my guide who works with me) to bring through a certain coloured ray to help in my client's healing. At the time it happens, about 50 percent of my clients comment that they can see the colour I have brought through. It always astounds me how this happens. I rarely tell my clients that I am bringing such a ray of colour to them. It is an instant and wonderful validation that my guide was correct. Afterwards, I usually gain further validation of how appropriate that ray of colour was for them, how peaceful, cleansed, or healed they felt.

You don't always have to have an energy healer do it for you; it is easy to learn to do it for yourself. Further on is a list of some of the rays of colour I have used with my clients and their healing qualities. You can add to the list what feels right for you or change my list to suit your personality and beliefs.

Healing Meditation Using Colour

Choose a colour that fits with your needs or that just simply feels right. Make sure you will not be interrupted. Turn off your phones. Put on some soft music that is slow and gentle with no words to distract you. Turn off electric lighting if you are doing it at night, and light candles to help bring the colour to you and to create the soft ambience needed for this kind of healing. If you like, place crystals of a similar colour at your side, or hold them in your hands. A bunch of flowers of similar colour is also lovely to have close by. In taking time to think about what would be nice for you to have around you, to "set the scene," if you like, you are putting into place a strong intention to heal and you are honouring your own soul-self.

It is better to sit upright, as you are going to bring the colour down through the top of your head. It may help you to record the following meditation so you don't have to be thinking about what comes next.

With your eyes open, take a few deep breaths to relax your whole body, all the while watching the flame of the candle. Concentrate on releasing all tension from your body. The less tense your body, the more powerful will be the healing. When you are feeling totally relaxed, close your eyes. Visualize coming from way, way up above your head the coloured ray you have chosen. See it come down through the top of your head. Take your time. See that ray fill your head, flow down into your neck, divide, and flow down both arms to the tips of your fingers. Then see that ray move down into your chest, filling it completely, and going through to your back. See it move down and fill your abdomen and middle to lower back. Then see it flow down into your hips, dividing and going down both legs to the tips of your toes. When you feel you have totally filled your body with that beautiful coloured ray, see it expand outwards into your energy field (about one to one and a half metres around you): in front of you, behind, below, above, and to the sides of you. Hold that ray of light for as long as you can. The more you practice, the longer you will hold the vision of that ray.

If you are confused as to what colour to use, then simply use pure white or golden light. White light holds all the colours. Should you find that you have chosen a particular colour but another one keeps coming in, allow the other colour to have its way and switch over to it, or allow both to be present. You may need to keep on doing this healing a number of times before you begin to feel its healing effects at a physical, mental or emotional level. As you commence the healing, become aware of a beautiful, loving being standing behind you in loving support for you.

When you feel the process has been completed for now, thank the being who was present with you and then Great Spirit for bringing this healing energy to you. I have found that genuine gratitude amplifies the healing process.

The Colours I Most Frequently Use

For mental healing, such as depression, anxiety, lack of trust and so on:

- Deep pink
- Medium blue
- Soft violet
- Pale green

For emotional healing, such as grief, broken heart, fear and so on:

- Deep pink
- Deep blue
- White

Healing for feeling powerless:

- Deep bright yellow
- White

For spiritual healing of the soul:

- Purple
- Magenta
- Cobalt blue

For sexual/sensual healing and for women wanting to have a baby:

- Apricot (combines orange of the sacral chakra and pink of divine love)

- Light and vibrant orange
- Deep and sparkling red (the red rose of love)
- Blue-green of sage (physical healing)

For physical healing of any kind:

- Emerald green
- Aqua (blue-green of the sea)
- Maroon (combines red and blue)
- White

Colour healing can in no way hurt you. There is no such thing as getting it wrong. Follow your gut level feeling; trust what colour you feel is right for you…..and *enjoy!*

When dealing with issues involving family, friends, study, or work that are causing stress and creating tension, choose a calming colour, such as a soft green, or blue, or pink, and do the above meditation. It will help to clear the jumble of thoughts, ease the feelings of fear and pain, and allow you to come into a calmer, clearer space to think through your problems.

If you are suffering from a physical or mental illness, then this meditation will aid the rest of the medical care you or your medical practitioner may have already chosen and begun for you. If you have doubts as to whether or not it will work, what harm is there in giving it a go? Working with colour is always a beautiful thing to do.

Explore and have fun with colour. Enjoy wearing colours you perhaps have been afraid to wear, and ask yourself what the different colours mean for you, and what part do they play in your healing. Be daring! Let go of your fears and work towards standing fully in your own beautiful energy as the delightful soul you truly are.

7 Breakdown Of Communication

THIS FAST PACE IN which we live, along with the incredible energies right around this planet at this moment in time, is having its effect on us.

Mother Earth is doing a massive cleansing which, at an ethereal vibrational level, is impacting upon us. Our energy fields are connected to the vibrational energy of our planet and, indeed, the cosmos. You know that saying 'We are all one!' That is the simple truth. Our energy fields are all interconnected. Hence, when Mother Earth cleanses herself, she presents us with the opportunity to do the same.

Think of it like this:

I can be having a fabulous day, high in energy, feeling happy, and then I meet someone who is depressed, and all of a sudden the sun has gone down. I am suddenly feeling tired and a little depressed myself. Why? Because their energy field is interacting with my energy field, and I am picking up on their depression and pain. They, on the other hand, are probably feeling heaps better because I have just given their energy field a boost. Those who live with someone who is depressed will tell you how "it drags them down." So when our lovely planet is going through major changes, such as fire, floods, volcanic eruptions and earthquakes, her energy field is disturbed and, in turn, is disturbing our energy field.

Where am I leading to with all of this? How many of us are going through major life changes, or self-exploration, or turmoil within relationships, or are questioning what life is all about? Just about everyone is going through their own cleansing, getting rid of the negative to make way for the positive.

Just as it is painful for people in the areas of disturbance, when Mother Earth does her spring cleaning, so can a time of cleansing and renewal be mighty painful for us as individuals. It is not easy letting go of the old to make way for the new. During these times, we may need to accept the help of others; another opinion, another perspective, other guidelines to get us through it all. It is, therefore, important for us to find the right person with whom we feel comfortable to share our burdens and to get a healthy perspective on our problems.

Finding the right therapist to help us can be a bit tricky. Just as it is with everyone else, therapist are human beings who can make mistakes. I often hear, "Oh, that therapist did nothing for me. They are not all that good at what they do. That's why I have come to you." As soon as I hear that statement I cringe. My immediate thought is, *so I wonder what you will say about me when you leave here!* It should always be a wake-up call for the therapist to stop and examine why the client and the previous therapist could not work together. There are several reasons why this may have been the case. I present a few for your consideration:

1. There is a personality clash. A client with a softer personality may require a more gentle way of being helped. A person with a strong personality may need a therapist who is more up-front with what they say. A really good therapist will

see what this person's personality requires and will adapt to accommodate their healing process.

2. The client may have simply been with a therapist who felt a little out of their depth with the client's problems. If this is the case, then the therapist needs to be honest with the client and recommend they see another therapist.

3. The client may have been withholding information and expecting the therapist to be a mind reader. This is something I occasionally encounter; when I do, I simply say, "A doctor can't help you to heal if you don't tell him what the symptoms are. If you are expecting me to help you, then I need to know what the problem is."

4. The client may have expectations of the therapist that are unreasonable. The role of a therapist is to help their clients help themselves, to give them an objective insight into their issues and present them with the means to deal with the issues and to step into the healing process. A therapist cannot heal their client. A therapist helps a client to heal himself or herself.

5. The therapist may be overworked and therefore tired and not have the clear-sightedness needed to handle their client's problem. It is essential for therapists to take breaks away from work; to rest and eat nutritious foods; to relax and have some fun. Dealing with other people's problems day after day can become a strain on the therapist, draining their energy. Clients should remember that the therapist is also human.

These are just a few of the more common reasons why communication between a therapist and their client breaks down. It does not necessarily mean that the therapist is bad at what they do (although there are always degrees of excellence in any profession). It may simply mean a wrong match between client and therapist. I have been to doctors who have been highly recommended to me by other people and wondered what those people saw in that doctor. However, that doctor is probably very competent with my friends, but he and I saw things differently. And so it is with any relationship in any area of our life.

For us therapists, if it is not working for us and our client, we need to be honest with them and say so. Either offer to do things differently or suggest they need to contact another therapist. This does not mean we are a failure, it simply means wrong person, wrong place, wrong time. We need to let go of it and know there are plenty of people we can help, and then there are always the few we will never be able to help. However, it is always a good practice to spend time examining self to see if we can improve our techniques.

For the client, remember that therapists are not gods, they are human beings with needs like ours, and the majority of them are deeply caring people who have our welfare at heart. If it is not working for us, then we need to seek out someone else with whom we can feel comfortable as we work through our problems and step into a healthier and happier life.

In conclusion, I share a story of a woman who came to see me a few years ago:

My new client opened her communication with me by saying that she had seen five other people, and they had all told her the same thing. And they were all wrong! I asked, "How can five people all be wrong? Perhaps you were not ready to hear what they had to say, or you didn't want to hear it." And guess what? Without knowing what the others had said, I told her the same thing! I have not seen her since.

When we are going through a time of change, upheaval, cleansing, and introspection, then let us allow it to bring a clearer path ahead with renewed vigour, a greater sense of self-worth, and a sense of excitement of what our future may hold for us.

8 Spirits Of The Ancestors

AS I WRITE, I gaze out my window to Earth Mother preparing for her time of rest. The autumn leaves are superb, such richness of colour, and the lush green of the grass is a balm to jaded nerves.

It has struck me how easily our Earth Mother lets go of that which no longer serves her; letting go of the old to make way for the new. Why, then, is it so hard for us to let go of the old to make way for the new? Earth does it with such grace and beauty, trusting that the joy of new life will be hers to experience again. She has much to teach us, this beautiful Earth Mother.

Let us not forget those beautiful spirits who so lovingly guard our land and help Earth on her journey through her seasons: the Earth angels we call fairies, and the spirits of the ancestors.

After my husband died, I sold our home, bought ten acres of land, and began to build a new home. During that time of creating my new home, a beautiful aboriginal spirit made himself known to me. I asked who he was, and he replied, "You may call me Billy. This is not my real name but the name the new people [white settlers] gave to me. This was once my home. We have gone, all of us, we have gone. I am now the spirit guardian of this land. I am in the land and the land is in me." I told Billy I was going to build a home on this land, but this home would also be a place of healing. I asked him to help me heal the land as I disturbed it to create this place of healing. I called this new home of mine *Tarilta*, aboriginal for "kangaroo."

As each tree was felled to make room for the house and dam, I asked of Earth Mother forgiveness for my actions and I promised Billy, and the realm of fairy, I would grow others in their place. There were few native birds when I first purchased the land. As I replaced the trees, I concentrated on planting shrubs that would attract birds, such as honeyeaters, wrens, and parrots. The birds came and were a constant source of amusement and joy to me. With the creation of the dam, there came a huge frog population and, of course, the lovely kangaroos.

Billy became a constant companion and dear friend. Each day my heart filled with gratitude for this beautiful friend, for his patience, kindness, and understanding of my intent to create beauty in and around that home.

Part of what I do is "house clearing," sending back to spirit those beings who are stuck in the astral plane, who are confused and upset, who want to go back to their soul family but are not sure how to do so. The astral plane is a band of energy around Earth, beginning at the Earth's crust, the soil, and moving out into the atmosphere. It is that which links the physical and ethereal planes.

People can sometimes choose to stay behind instead of going to the light and returning to their family in spirit. There are many reasons why they choose this path. Often an old person, who is worried about their partner, chooses to stay present in the house and watch over their loved one. Then when their partner dies and goes straight back to the soul family, the other partner gets stuck in that area immediately around us called the astral plane... hence our ghosts. They remain in that home, hotel, or place of business, lost and confused. Sometimes they are unaware that they have died and can become upset with others taking over "their home" and changing it.

However, there are others, such as Billy, who have been back to their soul family but decide to return to Earth in spirit form to do work of some kind, such as being a guardian of land that once was sacred to them.

I was asked to clear a hairdressing salon that had once been a home. Three people were present in spirit: a young European woman in her early thirties with a little girl by her side, and a man of aboriginal descent.

The hair salon had once been the home of the woman, who died in child birth. The little girl had died with her. She knew she was caught in the astral plane and was very ready and willing to return home. As I returned her to the light, it was lovely to see her welcomed home by the man who had been her husband. At long last they were together again. As she started to fade from view, she looked back at me and smiled.

The aboriginal man, on the other hand, had no desire to leave. He was guardian of the land upon which chemicals were being used. I told the owner of the salon [who was struggling to keep her business going and felt it had something to do with her unwanted visitors] what was happening and added that he did not wish to leave. Instead of coming into a place of understanding and reconciliation with him, she chose instead to say, in an angry way, "Tell him to go. Piss the bastard off!" There was a moment of shocked silence on my behalf, and then I quietly said, "Sorry, but no, I cannot do that. Do you not understand that he is protecting the premises? I cannot ask him to leave if he does not wish to do so."

All it would have taken for there to be peace and comfort in her place of work was the desire to connect with this beautiful being through a simple meditation and to ask him to understand what she was trying to achieve….helping women and men to step into their inner beauty by allowing themselves to take care of their outward appearance. She could have created a lovely working agreement between herself and the aboriginal man. She could have had the benefit of his protection and friendship. Instead, she chose the path of fear, anger, and resentment.

Fear is such a huge block between us and the realm of spirit. Fear is what will bring to us the negative experiences with spirit beings. *That which we think, we create.* If we choose instead to be in a place of friendship and love with these beings, then that is also what we create for ourselves.

I have since moved to another beautiful home. Again I sensed the presence of an ancestral guardian, as I moved around the property with the real estate man, making a decision to buy it. Sammy, the ancestor in spirit, was checking me out to see if he and I could happily coexist. In my mind, I smiled and told him I would be grateful if he would protect my new home and the land on which it was built. A nod of the head was his reply. Since then, Sammy and I have gotten to know each other in a quiet and gentle way. I asked his permission to give the home a name. Together we have called it *Balamara*. It is an aboriginal word meaning *"morning star,"* leading people out of their dark night into a new day. Again I feel my home and land are totally protected.

It is so important for us to thank the ancestors and guardians of our land [and hence our home] for the love and protection they bring, not only to the land but also to us.

35

9   *Does Hell Exist?*

DURING A WORKSHOP, I was asked what I thought life after death looked like, and what happens to people who have lived a life of a criminality or cruelty to other humans.

The conclusion I have come to for myself [it may differ greatly for others, so I can only speak for myself] is that such beings go to a place of accountability and healing. My conclusion comes from doing a huge amount of reading on the subject; having had two close encounters myself with death, and having worked with people who have had near-death experiences. But mostly my conclusion has come through my contact with the realm of spirit as a medium.

I do not believe in a place called hell! Hell is what we create here in our earthly existence. However, we all go through a life review. It is a time of learning how we could have done better and where we did well. There is no judgement as such. We are our own judges. Great Spirit's role with us is not about judgement but about love, healing, and teaching us so that we can learn, grow, and expand in our soul's evolution.

However, for those who have lived lives that have been destructive to other people as well as themselves [thieves, murderers, cruel people] before returning to their soul family, journey to a place where they are shown, in graphic detail, how damaging their lives have been both to others and to their own soul. In this place they also go through a process of cleansing and healing. They then go back to square one and begin their soul's evolution again. In some way, they make a commitment to counterbalance the karma they have created with that destructive life. In their next life they may come back as a healer of some kind, or seek a path of isolation to fully commit themselves to their spiritual journey, or maybe to teach music or art.

Justin, another participant at the same workshop, asked, "What about Hitler? What are your thoughts about him?" At the very moment Justin asked the question, a young Rosella parrot flew into the window and died. A powerful message from the animal world, important enough for one very beautiful bird to give its life for us to "get" it!

So what was the message? The first thing to remember was the bird was young. The second thing to realise is the bird thought it saw something that turned out to be an illusion [the mirror of the outside world in the window]. Because it believed in the illusion, it lost its life, and its dream of flying high was gone. See any likenesses to Hitler? Hitler began his political life as a fighter for the under dog, for the workers of Germany. His vision in his youthful days as a politician was to fight the establishment on behalf of the workers to get them fair pay for a fair day's work with good working conditions. And then he saw the illusion created by the negative side of his ego, the seductive, enticing feeling of power over the people, and eventually he "flew into the window" and lost his ability to fly high, and ultimately his life!

The same message can apply to our spiritual journey and to our inner growth. The ego is a clever little chap. It is so easy to step into judgement of others whom we perceive to be less spiritual than ourselves. Who are we to judge? We do not know the workings of that person's heart and mind. And anyway, what is spiritual judgement based on? For me, standing at the sink doing the dishes can be an act of spirituality.

When we, like Hitler, allow the negative ego to rule, we lose sight of reality and begin to believe the illusion, and when we do, we will surely fly into the window! It is so important, as we increase our growth and spiritual awareness, to be ever mindful that we do not have the right to judge what we do not know about another's journey with their soul.

I looked around the group in front of me and said, "Let's not kid ourselves. We too have been little Hitler's at some stage in our journey with past lives. We too have had a taste of the seductive illusion of power wrongly used. We would all like to think our past lives have been tragic at the hands of others, or that we have been magnificent beings of some kind. The truth is, most of us have slogged it out over many lifetimes, and some of them have not been pretty. I in no way condone what Hitler did, it was barbaric, but then so were some of the things done in the name of victory by our own politicians and armed forces. None of us are innocent when it comes to having allowed the negative ego to rule."

We thanked the bird for the powerful message it brought to us. In the middle of some amazing experiences and insights people were getting from participating in the workshop, Justin's question and the parrot's message brought a sobering, grounding energy into the room.

10 *The Seasons*

OUR ENERGY IS INTERCONNECTED with the energy of Mother Earth. Everything has a field of energy. This computer on which I am currently working, the desk on which it sits, the tree outside my window, the coffee I am drinking, the painting on the wall, every single thing upon this planet and within the universe has an energy field. We are literally one with all that is. Our energy field is merging with everyone and everything. Hence, we are divinely and intimately connected to Mother Earth and her seasons. Spring is about new growth, new adventures and renewal. Summer is about joyfulness and celebration, being at the height of one's energetic vibrations. Autumn is the time for release, the letting go of the old to make way for the new; a golden time. And winter?

Winter is the season of inner reflection and rest. We have much to learn from nature and the way Mother Earth responds to the winter season. But do we? Do we learn from this beautiful planet on which we live? It is the season of reflection and rest, but our society has forgotten how to let go and relax. We even feel guilty for taking time to be still, to allow ourselves to dream, to just simply *be*. So when winter challenges our immune system, and we are tense from work and family issues, unable to rest, to let go of the tension and relax, then we are vulnerable to all kinds of viruses.

Viruses love nothing better than a body that is tired, run down, grabbing food on the run, tense, pushed to its limit with socializing or work, with consuming more alcohol, cigarettes, and drugs than is good for it. Viruses love a body that is carrying around a person who is emotionally upset and mentally exhausted. Viruses love someone who thinks the world will fall apart if they are not there to be in control of what is happening, who think no one else can go on without them. In our full-on rush to create a life for self, we fail to care for and love this miracle called a body, this miracle that houses the essence of our being.

I am no exception. I have had a major lesson in believing the world cannot exist without me!

My ex-husband had returned from time away in Adelaide with a nasty throat, head, and chest virus. Both he and I had been through emotional and mental strain as we prepared to go our separate ways. Tension and grief had lowered the effectiveness of our immune systems. But I had to add another dimension to it all. As he walked in the door, I looked at him and said, "Okay, please stay away from me. I am booked out with clients. I can't afford to get ill. Sorry, but I do not need this virus. I have got the next three weeks filled with people who need to step into their own healing. Go to bed and don't breathe on me!" Compassionate, hey!

So guess what happened? Yep, I got the virus! Why? First thing I did was go into the negative thought pattern, "I don't want the virus," and in so doing put out the message that I believed I was going to get it! I already knew that I was in a place of tension and grief over the separation, but I couldn't allow that to be seen, could I? That would mean I was weak or something, right? And then, of course, the world could not go on without me nurturing it and helping it to overcome its multitude of problems, right? Wrong! I actually found the world does very well without me being there to rescue it. Every client rebooked, and they were not in the least upset that I could not see them. The old virus had a fantastic party with my not listening to what my body, mind, and heart were trying to say to me. Enforced rest is what it is called!

As I sat up in bed one morning, cup of coffee in hand, I decided to pull a card and see what it had to say about this virus. I took it from Osho's Zen Tarot pack. The card that came up was 7 of Fire – *Stress*. It says:

The quality of stress represented by this card visits all of us at times. We create it ourselves with the idea that without us nothing will happen, especially in the way we want it to! Well, what makes you think you're so special? Do you think the sun won't rise in the morning unless you personally set the alarm?

The message ended with a positive tone, but it was exactly the kick in the butt I needed. Later, I was able to see the virus as the special gift it was meant to be, the beautiful, uncomfortable, teacher!

We need to love ourselves enough to know we too need nurturing. We need give ourselves permission to simply *be*, to do nothing but dream, to rest, to relax, and let go of the incredible pace of life we have all got caught up in. Mother Nature indeed has much to teach us. And for those who are going through major life changes, be gentle with yourself, and be honest about needing time out just for you.

There is only so much we can pour out of a jug before it has to be refilled.

11   *The Creative Self*

ONE OF THE QUESTIONS I am often asked is, how do you write? Do you sit down and write every day, or do you just write when you are inspired? I believe it is a question that most writers grapple with from time to time.

The simple truth is, the only thing that will stop us from becoming successful writers, artists, singers, or performers of any kind [or carpenters or business men/women] is our own lack of self -worth and self-esteem. We all make a choice to take a risk and step into the flow of success or to remain in the safety of the mundane.

In 2011 and 2012, I attended the You Can Do It seminars in Melbourne. One of the things that stood out for me was that every single one of those people who spoke had known painful experiences and hardship in their earlier life. None of them came from a background of ease. Each one of them has been through trauma of some kind that would see others giving up on themselves. But these spiritual giants believed in their journey to bring peace and happiness to this planet in their own unique and individual way. They saw the trauma they have been through as their testing ground to stand up for self, to believe in self, and to learn huge and valuable lessons through those experiences.

For a few moments on the first day, I sat listening to these people deliver their powerful messages, shrinking into my seat with thoughts of, *Oh for heaven's sake Joy, how do you think you could possibly do what these people are doing? Who do you think you are to have thoughts of being in their place?* Ironic, hey! Here I am at a You Can Do It seminar, and I am sliding off in the opposite direction.

It is a trap we all fall into at some time in our life's journey. Even these great people have been down that road. The simple truth is, when we step out of the negative ego/mind self and step into our soul-self, there is absolutely nothing we cannot achieve. We are one with and a part of Great Spirit, and Great Spirit is one with and a part of us. Who are we to deny Great Spirit the right to work with us and through us for the greater good of our planet? Why should I think I can't do it when I have been given gifts to be used for the benefit of my fellow human beings in distress?

On the second day, I had the wonderful opportunity to spend a few moments with John Holland. As I am, John is a psychic medium, communicating with beings in the realm of spirit. I have always admired this man and the way he works. What I found, of course, was a very humble and beautiful human being. We stood as equals, chatting about his work and mine. I felt I had known him a long time. And the thought ran through my head: we do these people a disservice by placing them on pedestals, removing them from our normality, and we do our own soul a disservice by not seeing that we too can be great in our own way. A gentle insight rose in me like a soft pink dawn. We are all here to learn a singular lesson: how to live a joyful life, so, too, are we all meant to step into our greatness.

I have listened to people lecture on the art of writing; I have gone to workshops on how to write; I have sat with my own guilt because I was not doing what they told me I had to do to become a successful writer. The simple truth is, we either want to write seriously for publication or we just want to have fun with it. The choice is ours, and there is no right or wrong to it. The secret is in our intention. I have been told by professional writers that you must write something every day or you are not a serious writer, and you will never be a good one. Well, I wasted a great deal of time sitting looking at a blank piece of paper or a blank screen with a blank mind and asking, "Okay! So, what are we going to write about, Joy?"

How one operates as a beautiful creative being is as individual as the number of people on this planet. There is no right or wrong. It is about finding out for ourselves how best we can operate to gain the maximum out of our gifts. I have written poems on toilet paper, notes of inspiration on paper napkins in restaurants, phrases on paper bags, and even a poem for a wedding on a wrapper off a Subway take-away. The edges of newspapers are great for writing down inspired thoughts.

When I am inspired to write, I turn off the phones and lock my doors. I make no excuses for locking myself away, after all, what I write in that time is hopefully for the greater good of future readers. I make no excuses when I need to close off from the world to create. The world will wait for me. When the urge to create fills my mind and heart, I let nothing stand in my way!

I am often asked, "What is writer's block? And how can I break through it?" The truth is simple. Writers' block means a tired brain. When we get writers' block, we need to switch off the brain and give it a holiday. Stop thinking about what you are meant to be writing. Go for a walk, dig in the garden, go for a swim, or watch a crazy movie. Do anything but write. Writer's block means your brain is trying to tell you it is tired and needs a break.

And most of all, get rid of the guilt! Guilt for any reason never serves us well.

This, of course, not only applies to writers; it can apply to any aspect of our life. "You can do it" is a great mantra. It helps us to believe in ourselves. When we believe in ourselves, our world changes for us. Remember, what we believe, we create! The saying is as ancient as man and is perhaps more relevant today than it ever has been. It is the old law of attraction. We reap what we sow; that which we give out comes back to us; what we believe, we create. So if I believe I cannot be as great as these amazing people, then I won't be. If I believe I am one and part of the same magnificent energy called God, Great Spirit or whatever name one cares to call that energy, then greatness is mine for the believing and asking. We are the drivers of our cars called life. We can put our foot on the acceleration pedal and move forward or stay right where we are. The choice is yours; the choice is mine. We can do it…or not!

12 *Are They With Me?*

THESE ARE SOME OF the most common questions I am asked as a medium:

- What is happening for my loved one?
- Are they okay?
- How can I have contact with them?
- How do I know they are with me?

The simple answer to "Are they okay?" is yes. When we die, regardless of how that death occurs or what our life was like prior to death, beyond that curtain of death we all walk through, there is only healing and love. There is no judgement and no place called hell. Hell is what we create here on this planet through our negative thoughts and feelings.

We all go through a life review that allows us to see where we could have improved and where we did brilliantly in our journey through this particular life. It is not a time of judgement, it is a time of learning. We return to being who we truly are beyond death. We are soul beings of light and love. We are joyously reunited with our soul family, for we have truly come *home* to them. We retain our personality, our memories, and the essence of who we really are. Time and time again, when I see people in the realm of spirit, I can describe what they looked like in their human form but, more importantly, I can describe their personality.

The question "Can I have contact with them and how do I know they are with me?" can also be answered simply. But the question that needs to be asked before that contact is made is, Are *you* ready for such contact? Our loved ones in spirit are usually with us and want the contact as much as we do [perhaps at times they want it more than we do]. They will go to extraordinary lengths, exerting a great amount of energy, to ensure that contact is made. The blockage in the contact happening is more likely to be with us than with them. If we have negative feelings towards those who have died, such as anger and resentment, our loved ones in spirit will quietly step back and remain silent until we are ready.

Before we say that our loved one is not with us, we need to question ourselves and see how prepared we actually are for that contact to be made. Over and over again, I get from my clients, "Why isn't my loved one around me? I don't feel their presence. And anyway, if they do come how will they appear?" The underlying feeling and the unspoken thoughts in these statements are that of fear. Fear of what we will actually encounter is the biggest block to having contact with a loved one. Our loved ones in spirit will always honour and respect where we are at in our journey with them. So if we say, "Show me a sign that you are with me, but don't show me a ghost because I am afraid of what I might encounter," then our loved one will respect our fear and walk ever so gently with us, to the degree that we may not be able to feel their presence.

All too often we try to control the process because of that fear. We often ask of our loved ones to appear in a specific way and therefore limit their ability to get through to us. We may be so vague about what we want from them, or ignorant about how it all works, that we miss the signs that they are using to try to get through to us.

So here are some examples of how our loved ones may try to send messages to us [we need to remain grounded as we begin to seek out such messages]. For example; our loved one may use feathers to let us know they are with us [however not all feathers will be a message from them]. It works more like this: we may be making the bed and look down to see a feather at our feet; we come home from shopping and there is a feather on the doormat; we may be doing the dishes and see a feather sitting near the fruit bowl. Not all feathers will be a message from our loved ones, but those found in unusual places are likely to be a gift of love from them.

Here are some other ways in which they may try to make contact:

- The words of a song or words that stand out from a page in a newspaper.
- A feeling of someone touching us, such as a hand on the shoulder, a hand running through our hair, a hand on our leg as we are going to sleep.
- Smells, such as Mother's perfume, Father's pipe tobacco, husband's aftershave, auntie's chocolate, floral scent from those who loved their roses or jasmine, shavings of wood from carpenters. Smells are unlimited. Trust what you get.
- Butterflies, dragonflies, or ladybird beetles are common ways of receiving messages. Now, not all butterflies are going to be a message from loved ones, but one that lands on your hand or shoulder or that keeps on circling around you probably is.
- Dreams are the easiest way for loved ones to come to us. When we awake from a dream where we have been in contact with a loved one, it is easy to say it was just a dream. Know that our loved ones try hard to get through to us, to let us know we are not alone and that they are there for us. [See chapter 21, "Dreams or Visions?"].
- Day dreams are also a good way for loved ones to make themselves known. We may be sitting having a cup of tea,

gazing out the window, and we suddenly feel their presence and see a vision of them in our mind.

There are many ways in which our loved ones will try to get through to us. They have a tough job at times, especially when they have made a clear connection, such as in a dream, and we then say, "Oh, that was just my imagination." Can you imagine their frustration?

The two things that will allow contact to be made with a loved one:

- Trusting what we get
- Letting go of fear and control

It is rare to see a loved one as a spirit form. Occasionally, they may appear as a light blue or white misty haze, especially at night, just before we drop off to sleep. Jeff, my lovely deceased husband, was great at using the movement of air, typically blowing papers out of my hand, especially papers that may have had some relevance to him, such as his death certificate or poems he loved to read. One day my Jeff showed himself to one of my friends:

We had been to a restaurant for lunch and had just stepped outside to go to our cars and leave. As we were saying good-bye, a sudden small whirlwind blew up behind me. When my friend looked over my shoulder, she suddenly turned pale. When I asked what was wrong, she said, "I just saw a man in that whirlwind behind you!" She then described him; clearly, it was my Jeff. He is a very playful spirit. I laughed, for it was typical of his ability to use the elements of nature.

There was a shocked silence when I explained to my friend who he was and why he had used the whirlwind to make his appearance. I don't think she will ever forget that moment in her life.

Jeff had been a man of the Earth, a sailor during World War 11 and then a forest officer. As a forest officer, he had been one of Australia's experts in bushfire behaviour and control. The direction and velocity of wind had always played a major part in his work.

Our loved ones want to talk to us as much as we want to talk to them. When we let go of fear, trusting that they are doing all they can to reach us, then we open the way for them. Our loved ones also want us to move through our grief and to reclaim our happiness. Our pain is their pain. They don't want us to remain stuck in that painful place, nor do they want us to feel guilty for letting go of them and allowing ourselves to enjoy life again. Our pain not only prevents us from moving forward, but it may also inhibit them.

In my book, *When Do The Tears Stop?,* I told the story of how Jeff came through to me when I was ill with influenza. He lovingly reprimanded me for clinging to the past instead of allowing myself to live in the present and look to the future. My pain was his pain. Whilst I held on to pain, neither of us could move forward. In that book, I have shared some simple ways in which I was able to release the pain and reclaim my happiness.

Death is not the end, it is a new beginning, a new way of being for both the one who has died and the one left behind. We can shut ourselves down and sit in the pain and loneliness for the rest of our lives. Or we can work through the pain to explore a new life and a new way of being. Sometimes, a fear of the unknown and sitting in the pain of grief can prevent us from creating a magical and beautiful life for ourselves.

13 *Awakening To Self*

WATCHING PEOPLE UNFOLD TO themselves, I am constantly in awe of how beautiful people can be when they fully step into their divine self.

When people come together (particularly during my workshops) with the intent to expand in self-awareness, to open up and acknowledge the beauty within, miracles begin to happen. With the expansion into self-awareness comes the desire to reach out and touch the lives of others with love. After someone puts their hand up and says a big *yes* to allowing self to step forward into becoming an awakening soul, within hours I see a fabulous shift from lack of confidence into a powerful and divine being. I always walk away from my workshops with a deep feeling of gratitude to my beautiful ones in spirit for the wisdom and knowledge that was imparted to these students of life. That which you teach, you also learn and experience, and so it is for me as I work with both humanity and divinity.

Workshops are a wonderful way to kick-start our growth, our awareness, and are wonderful ways for us to learn, to expand our minds, and to think laterally. But we do not need to wait for a workshop to appear, for a teacher to guide us, to step into who we truly are. That process begins now, in this very moment, and continues to be a moment by moment experience for the rest of our lives. There is no end to the learning. How can there be? We are eternal beings who have come a long way in our journey and still have a long way to go.

We have all experienced the tough times. Life is moving at such a fast pace. With that fast pace comes challenges that can be difficult. But let us see them for what they are: experiences from which we can learn so much about ourselves, discovering yet another layer to our inner strength and courage.

We need to let go of sitting in the pain, of standing in the shadows of those experiences. Instead, we need to take from them the moments of beauty, of inner growth, that allows us to expand into our greater self. Never waste a tough experience by sitting in self-pity. See it for what it is:

It is a blessing through which we learn more about self and the power of self-loving and self-acceptance.

Dr John F Demartini in his book *The Breakthrough Experience*, says:

I believe we have a mortal self and an immortal self, a part of us that's run by the outer world and a part that's called by the inner world. To the degree that we listen to the inner voice and vision rather than the outer, we awaken our immortal genius and inspiration. The word genius comes from the Latin root meaning 'guardian spirit', and that is exactly what great teachers and immortal thinkers are: creative, guardian spirits who shine light on what seems dark to others. Our own soul is the ultimate guardian spirit, and a genius is one who listens to their soul and obeys.

There are so many wonderful people out there writing so many wonderful books. Why not go and find them!

14 One With The Cosmos

WE TEND TO FORGET we are part of a greater plan that involves our solar system, our galaxy, and the never-ending cosmos. We are a tiny part of that system, the proverbial drop in the ocean, but a most important part. In our own solar system we are the only planet with water on it: that oh, so precious thing called water. Because we have water, we are the only planet to have our kind of life: thousands of species of trees, birds, animals, insects, fish, reptiles, and such a huge variation in human beings. This tiny planet called Earth in this solar system is a miracle that we take so much for granted.

There is, I believe, a greater plan we cannot see, a shift in cosmic energy coinciding with the shift in humanities awareness and soul growth. Many people, self included, have been going through years of sorting out issues, saying good-bye to loved ones as they return home to their soul families, and overcoming difficulties of all kinds. I believe it is a shifting of negative energy to prepare for the new era that is upon us.

This era does not begin with a date; there is no defining line. The era has already begun and has been with us for some time as the old energy fades out and the new quietly slips in, overlapping each other. And what is this new era? It is a time of love and peace. Nice words, yes? Regardless of the energy of the cosmos and its amazing endurance with us humans, this time of love and peace cannot be fully realised unless the people of this planet want love and peace in their minds and in their hearts. I hear you ask, is that not what everyone wants?

Love and peace begin within us. When, as a collective race called mankind, we begin to truly understand the reasons why we have free will and an ego:

- We understand that the ego is our greatest teacher and free will comes with great responsibility
- We understand that we truly want to understand and love self
- We understand that we yearn deep inside ourselves to want to love all of our fellow mankind and this planet on which it is a privilege to live

Only then can the full energy of love and peace sweep across this planet of ours.

Without our deliberate participation in love of self, love of others, and love of our planet, regardless of how much the cosmos is trying to herald in this new energy of love and peace, it will be lost in the flow of people's negative thoughts and emotions. We need to actively participate in bringing that positive, loving energy to our planet if it is to succeed.

Every thought has energy; every emotion has energy. Imagine what that must look like if someone out in space could physically see that energy field around Earth, the collective energy of all our thoughts and emotions! If everyone on the planet at any given moment was having a negative thought and experiencing a negative emotion, Earth would be surrounded by this murky, thick fog of negativity. Now reverse that process. If everyone at any given moment was thinking beautiful thoughts and feeling love for self and everyone else, now that would be a very different picture our friend out in space would be seeing. It is our job as individuals to help the cosmic energy make that shift to peace and love a reality.

Mostly we do not understand the power of our thoughts either in our own life or how they affect everyone around us. Take a look at successful world leaders: both of Gandhi's in India (prime minister and fighter for human rights), Nelson Mandela, King Arthur, Martin Luther King - the list is endless. What do they all have in common? They all believed in themselves.

When we begin to love self and believe in self, we step into helping the cosmos begin that huge shift from a negative energy field, created by humans, to a positive one of love and peace worldwide. How we operate on this planet also has its effect on the cosmos. There is no separation. We are one with all that *is*.

It is a simple truth: the new age of love and peace begins inside us as individuals seeking out our soul's purpose, connecting to our higher self, and coming into healing of all past negative experiences. In so doing, we step into love for self, for our fellow human beings, and for this amazing planet on which we live. When we begin with self, again as the important drop in the ocean, we all add to the beautiful cosmic energy. We add love for our planet, our solar system, and our galaxy.

Our greatest teachers are those who bring to us the greatest challenges. Instead of having negative thoughts and feelings toward them, try thanking them for the opportunity to learn to be strong, to stand up for self, to understand our own life purpose, and to discover self-acceptance and self-love.

One of my greatest teachers was my deceased husband, Jeff. We were together for twenty-four years. I loved him dearly, as he loved me, but when it came to matters of my psychic ability and spirituality, there was great resistance from him. Through his resistance, I found my inner strength to hold on to my belief. Instead of convincing me I was wrong in my beliefs, Jeff unwittingly helped me to find my inner courage to hold on to what I knew was right for me. After he died, he came to me through another medium [someone I had never met before] and apologised for not believing me. With a laugh he said, "I believe you now."

As Nelson Mandela, that great South African fighter for human rights, justice, and equality, once said, "What others think of me is none of my business." What is our business is how we think and feel about our own self. We cannot change what others think of us, but we can change how we feel and think about ourselves.

At the end of my first marriage, I looked in the mirror and said to my reflection, "I hate you. I hate who you have become. I hate the ugliness inside your head. I hate your body. Where is the love I so wanted?" A quiet whisper came back to me: "I am still here. I am your soul that is complete love. I am still here waiting for you to see me!"

When we get to know our higher self in a more intimate way [connecting to our soul's life purpose, consciously working to change negative thoughts and feelings into loving ones], then we have more love for self and for those who participate in our life.

15 *Imperfection*

ANNE WAS A FABULOUS artist who never allowed her self to step into her greatness. Anne lived with fear and became an alcoholic.

Not long before Anne died, she said to me, "Joy, my loyal friend, write about me when I am gone. Use my experience to show others what not to do. Let others learn from my negative experience. In this way my life will not have been fully wasted." As I write, I feel my lovely soul friend standing beside me. I see her smile lighting up her beautiful eyes.

Whilst hanging her watercolours in my new home, I pondered on imperfection, how it can drive some people to constantly strive for perfection and how it can pull others down into depression, as it did for Anne. It is a choice we make: to stand in the light of our gifts or to sit in the darkness.

Imperfection is a gift if we allow ourselves to see it as such. Without imperfection, we would never expand and grow, reaching for our greatness. Artists of any kind are never fully satisfied with their achievements. Writers, painters, dancers, singers, photographers: they all live with the knowledge that they can do better. It never ends, this knowledge of imperfection in what we do, and neither should it.

The shadow of imperfection is what allows us to see the light of our potential.

As night allows us to appreciate and enjoy the day, as day allows us to appreciate and enjoy the night, so does our shadow side [that which is controlled by the mind] allow us to see our inner divine light [that which is controlled by the heart and soul]. We need to see our shadow side as a wonderful gift, to thank it for showing us the light. If Anne had seen her imperfection as a gift, rather than sitting in its darkness, then I have no doubt that she would have become a great artist.

But then, for Anne [as it is for some] her shadow was her comfort. It was her cave, like snuggling under a blanket during the night to shut out the world, to close off to her potential, to draw the blanket over her head so she could not see the light. To step into the light, to become the great artist deep inside she knew she was, meant taking risks. To stand tall in a critical world, a world where the talents of an artist are judged by people who do not understand the workings of her heart and mind, was a risk she could not allow herself to take.

It takes courage to stand in our greatness. It takes strength and determination to step out of the night into a new day. It means being true to one's self, honouring who we are and loving ourselves. The path is not always easy; people don't always understand. The hurdles can be difficult to climb over, but oh, what joy and fulfilment is our reward when we allow ourselves to step fully into our soul self, into our light, into our greatness. And how the heavens rejoice when we do!

Greatness has many faces. It is self-destructive to compare our greatness to that of others. The moment we do, we will lose it. Sometimes, greatness is a quiet and gentle thing that reaches out and softly touches another's heart.

My wonderful mother taught me about greatness just by being who she was. She was the last of eleven children to die. Imagine that: my mother experienced the grief of her parents and ten siblings all dying before her. She also went through five operations for cancer. She overcame two major strokes, where she lost the use of her speech and right arm and leg, both times, and both times she fought back. And in the midst of all of this, I would hear my mother singing as she did the ironing for her six children and husband. My mother never hit the headlines for her greatness, her courage, and her strength, but there are few who could equal her greatness in my eyes. She taught me by just being my mother.

Think about taking time out now, just for you, time to contemplate what greatness you could achieve, how you can expand and grow. Allow yourself time to commune with the soul, your spirit, through meditation, listening to music, going for gentle walks, riding your bike, or in any other way that allows you to become introspective and in tune with the essence of who you truly are.

And remember:

It is our imperfection that shows us our greatness. Without our imperfection, we would never know how great we can become.

16 Limitations

RECENTLY I WENT TO an art gallery with a friend to see an amazing exhibition of art work by another dear friend of mine, Tamara Bekier. It was a retrospective exhibition of the past thirty years of Tamara's gift as an artist. Tamara is now in her eighties, with a most incredible journey behind her. Born in Russia, she survived the awful, hellish trauma of a war camp in Germany; she migrated to Australia when the World War 11 ended and became an Australian citizen. Tamara began her career as an artist when she was fifty years old by enrolling in a degree course in fine arts.

Knowing the history of the hell Tamara had lived through, it was a total joy for me to walk amongst her creations and to see the vibrancy of her work, the beauty of her soul on paper and canvas. Tamara could have sunk to the depths of depression with all that she has been through. Instead, she chose to explore her gift as an artist and to share with the world her inner beauty.

This exhibition was not just one room full of work; it expanded into three big rooms, two small rooms, a hall, and at the top of the gallery, into what used to be an infirmary. There were over four hundred pieces of art. The thought hit me, as I wandered around absorbing the powerful messages that flowed through her work, how incredibly healing this has been for Tamara, and not only for her but for every person who allowed her work to speak to them. Having Tamara's work in the former infirmary seemed extremely appropriate.

We are all beautifully gifted beings. We may not see our gifts. We may choose to ignore them. We may decide they are unworthy of other people's attention, but it does not change the fact that we, too, are gifted and that gift could be powerful healing medicine.

Why limit one's self? So many times I see gifts in my clients that they are totally unaware of having. When I tell them what I see, I am usually met with, "Oh you have got to be kidding. Me? A singer [or artist or a writer]? I don't think so!" It saddens me that people limit themselves by not exploring the possibilities of the gifts with which they were born.

Is it not worth a try to explore the possibility of being a gifted and creative being? Who knows, we may discover a creative gift we did not realise existed. Think about the fun one can have exploring what may lurk beneath the surface of our conscious awareness, and how powerfully healing that would be. And when we heal ourselves, we also help to heal the world in which we live, as does Tamara.

It is fun thinking beyond the known self. It can be such a joyful moment, exploring the possibilities of being a creative and gifted being. Perhaps it would be nice to take time to question self and ask of self, "If I would like to be gifted in some creative way, what would I really like to do?" Who knows, we may open a new and exciting chapter in our book of life. And we may help ourselves to heal and, in doing so, help others to heal too. It is lovely to let go of limitations, to take a deep breath and allow self to expand into wholeness.

After all, we are beautiful souls, spirit beings, part of and one with the cosmos and Great Spirit!

17 *Judgement Or Assessment?*

I HAD VISITED THE local police station with some documents I needed signed. There was a line of people waiting. No one spoke. The atmosphere in the room was tense with unspoken thoughts.

When the process was completed, I looked at the officer, a man in his mid to late fifties, and said, "You blokes must get bored having to do this paper work when there are other activities you probably prefer to be doing. How many of your signatures have you put onto pieces of paper throughout your time in the police force?" He broke out into a big and delightful smile and blushed.

They were simple words, but they seemed to have a powerful impact. I walked to my car and sat for a few moments, pondering what had just taken place. I realised that day after day, these people perform these tasks and probably rarely get acknowledged for what they do.

Coming home from Melbourne one night, I shared a taxi with a man taking the same route as me. The conversation between the taxi driver and the other passenger was the kind I often hear.

"Any cops about mate? They're all bastards. You'd think they'd have enough to do without collecting revenue for the state. I got caught the other night. Jezz, I was only doing 5 over the 60. I asked him why he wasn't out chasing bloody

criminals. I'm glad he didn't ask me to breathe into his breathalyser though. I'm not sure if I would have been over the limit or not."

These two simple incidents got me thinking about how easily we can judge a group of dedicated and caring people by the antics of a few. Police, doctors and nurses, politicians, teachers; we judge without thought for the human factor in these people, the long hours they work, often doing arduous jobs. To say that all cops are bastards is actually not true. Neither is it true to say all doctors are unfeeling or incompetent. As a society, we have taken away from these people their right to be human beings: the right to be tired, to be stressed, to be affected by the people they are dealing with every day of their working lives, to feel pain and anger and love.

At home, cup of coffee in hand, I asked of myself, "What is the difference between judgement and assessment? Where is the line between the two? At what point during assessment do I step over the line into judgement?"

In truth, when I judge another in a negative way, I place myself on a pedestal. I am saying, "I am better than you." Sipping my coffee, I saw that any judgement I make actually comes from a vulnerable place within me, a place of needing to feel better than the other, needing to be right so that I feel okay as a person. If I put you down, I can build me up. It was a moment in my life when a light went on and exposed the untidy room in my mind that could do with a good clean. It was an uncomfortable moment of truth.

I think perhaps what works for me is this:

- Judgement is about making a situation, yourself, or someone else right or wrong
- Assessment is more about an evaluation of a situation, yourself, or someone else

I then took the thought a step further to how we judge as a society. Perhaps the time has come for all of us to learn to be more appreciative of the services given to us, to be less judgemental of those who provide those services, and to develop a greater understanding of the pressures and tensions with which these people live. But to change society's way of thinking towards groups of people begins with self.

I smiled at a policeman and complimented him on his work. He smiled back at me. It takes little effort to smile. Now I have fun exploring this way of being. It is amazing how a few words can change a whole situation. I love to see a smile light up the face of a person working at a supermarket check-out. When I spread sunshine, sunshine comes back to me. When my mood is heavy with worry, I always get the red lights, the sullen person behind the counter, or the crazy driver who doesn't give way, and I boil the milk over.

When I allow myself to be deeply honest with self, I realise that when I make something someone else's fault, it is usually because I am standing in judgement of self. This kind of self-judgement leads to low self-esteem.

Self-assessment, on the other hand, can be a very positive thing to do. The assessment of how we behave, our thoughts and what we say, how we react to what other's are saying, our feelings toward self all lead to self-evaluation and growth. When we can be honest with who we are and how we are developing, then we allow room for improvement. With improvement comes a higher self-esteem. With a higher self-esteem comes a deeper understanding of and caring for our fellow human beings.

It becomes a circle, and it all begins with self. That which happens in our outer world is a reflection of what is happening in our inner world. When we can learn to see the correlations between our outer world and our inner world, then we will grow and expand in a deeper, quicker, and healthier way.

The Master Jesus said, "Judge not, that ye be not judged!" (King James Bible: Matthew 7:1) In other words, what we give out comes back to us. I believe the master's message was twofold. I believe he was not only talking of the judgement of others but also of self-judgement.

18 *Unconditional Love*

MY FATHER, MY FIRST husband, my second husband, my lover, and my friend; these five men have taught me what unconditional love truly means. But it was my mother, bless her, who set the high example for me to follow, how to live in a state of unconditional love. I hear that phrase thrown around in conversations, and I question within me if the people who have uttered it realise what they have said.

To reach a state of truly loving in an unconditional way is to love expecting nothing in return. To love unconditionally means not wanting to change the person from who they are to who we would like to see them become. It is about asking for that which is for the other's highest good regardless of where that leaves us in their life. This has been a tough lesson for me to learn. I have been aware for a few years now that to love unconditionally is a major lesson for me in this life time.

I share the following experiences with you, believing that you may find some correlation to them in your life. Perhaps these experiences will help you to understand your own more fully.

MY FATHER

For the majority of my life, my father and I struggled with our relationship. I was the unwanted child, and in many ways throughout my life as a child, teenager, and young woman, my father demonstrated his wish that I had not been born. Later I came to understand why, but during those young years, the pattern of seeking my father's approval, and never receiving it, was set in concrete inside my heart.

My mother had just turned forty-one when I was born. My father had reached the point of believing that his time with children was finished. My conception was a shock to him and became a heavy burden in his heart.

Dad was eighty-four years old before our struggle was resolved, and it came in a painful way. My mother, throughout her life, had a series of serious illnesses: cancer, kidney problems, high blood pressure, and finally a series of strokes. After her final stroke at eighty-eight years of age, she could no longer be cared for by Dad in the family home. I spent a week with them, looking for a home for the elderly where she could live, and be cared for, in a safe environment. Dad was in no emotional place, knowing he was losing his mate, to sit still with her and be strong for her. That role fell to me. During that time, my father saw qualities in me he had not seen before, because he had been too busy rejecting my existence.

Through my mother's suffering came the healing between my father and me. Through his tears and anguish, the fearful and vulnerable man could be seen. It touched a rawness in my heart. We cried together, were honest with each other about our past, spoke our truth, and heard each other. For the first time he held me and hugged me in the way I had been asking for all of my life. In that moment, I understood that my hunger for his affection and my judgement of him had added to the barrier between us. Just prior to this event, I had decided to let go of being able to know fully my father's love.

The irony of it all slapped me. When I let go of wanting my father's love, it came to me. When I let go of my judgement of him, he let go of his judgement of me. When I decided to step into trying to understand what stood between us, he decided to try and understand what stood between us. In seeing his vulnerability, he saw mine. That which we give out is that which we receive. It was a major lesson in learning to love for love's sake and not because I wanted love to flow back to me.

At ninety-seven, my father decided he needed to leave his body and return home, to where his wife waited for him, [she had died some nine years previously]. Over a period of five weeks, he starved himself to death. During that time, I had a chance to let my father know how much I loved him. For me they were some of the most precious days of my life. Together we shared, in a deeply honest way, the healing of each other's hearts.

MY FIRST HUSBAND

We were married for eight years, and what a rugged ride was that journey we took together. For me, they were eight years of anger, bitterness, resentment, rejection, and misunderstandings. They were years of financial and emotional struggle. The greatest blessings were our two children, and what price have they paid for their parents' mistakes.

There was little love left between us by the time we had immersed ourselves in self-pity, self-judgement, and judgement of each other. There was little self-esteem left. I would look in the mirror and hate who I had allowed myself to become. My struggle with feelings of worthlessness, depression, loneliness, fear, and the ugliness of my thoughts brought me to my knees. When the separation came, it was a relief for both of us. No longer did we have to snarl at each other or ignore the other's presence.

Over the months that followed, I faced up to the part I had played in the downfall of our marriage. This marriage had brought to the surface the screaming little girl who ached to be held and loved; the child throwing tantrums because she was not heard or understood; the unwanted one who was a burden; the witch-bitch screaming at the world as the flames of judgement lapped around her feet; the teenager shedding tears of hopelessness.

As a clearer understanding of what we had done to each other seeped in, I came to realise that I had been asking the impossible of my husband. I tried to change him into the man *I* wanted him to be. After eight years of failing, I finally got the message: it was not my place to try and change anyone. What arrogance on my behalf to believe I knew what was best for him, that I knew better than he whom he should be. Nor could he fill the emptiness inside me and hold the child that needed to be comforted and loved. Only a deeper understanding of self and love for self could heal that festering childhood wound.

As weeks turned into months, and a deeper understanding grew within me, I began to let go of the bitterness and anger. A gentle kind of love for him, like that of a sister, began to erase the pain of separation and the awful sense of failure I felt as a woman and a wife.

I began to take the first steps in my next lesson in unconditional love: to love someone without wanting to change who they are. Many years after our divorce, he remains a friend. Thankfully, I am no longer the woman I was then. Years of personal growth and awakening to who I am has allowed me to see the beauty in him.

MY SECOND HUSBAND

Jeff and I had almost twenty-five years together. When he died, my world crumpled around me.

I was his princess, his lover, his confidante, his friend, his playmate. I was his joy and he was mine! We travelled the world, and we travelled inside each other's minds and hearts.

But walking hand in hand with the wonder was the darkness.

He was twenty-three years older than me and had spent four years as a sailor in World War 11. He suffered from what they used to call war neurosis; now they call it posttraumatic stress disorder. Whatever name you care to call it, its real title is *hell in the mind!*

And so began another lesson in unconditional love: learning to love someone in their deepest and darkest moments, without taking what they say and do as a personal affront, allowing them to walk through their darkness without judgement and with full understanding of the anguish within them. In those moments, I learned to put self aside for the good of another, and I learned that gentle persuasion and tenderness could quickly quell the roaring beast.

I found the greatest effect in silencing the beast was to go into my inner stillness, detach from the drama, and allow myself to be in a place of fearless love. Even in the blackest room, if you light a little candle, the darkness cannot exist.

So many times I held Jeff in my arms as he sobbed, this powerful man calling himself a murderer. Jeff had many damaging experiences, but the one that haunted him the most was the death of a young Japanese soldier. During a particular battle, Jeff had jumped into a bunker and immediately realised he was not alone. The Japanese soldier had got there first. It was kill or be killed. After, Jeff went into shock. His thoughts that followed were, *I have just killed someone's son, someone's husband, and maybe someone's father. Why am I doing this?* No matter how much I tried to tell him he was fighting for his country's freedom, that singular thought, *I am a murderer,* haunted him everyday of his life.

I didn't know when I married him what darkness existed in his mind, what hell was being experienced in his heart. I am thankful

I didn't, for I may not have married him. If I hadn't married him, I would have missed out on a wonderful experience. He loved me like a princess. I would have missed the privilege of holding someone in complete love as he trusted me enough to share his blackest moments.

Because of Jeff, I learnt to stand strongly and fearlessly in what is usually regarded as the male energy of strength and courage, allowing my inner power to grow, standing fully in my truth.

He is at peace now, held in the arms of true unconditional love.

MY LOVER

When I was fifty-nine, my lover came to me, filling my life with sunshine when the pain of loss following Jeff's death was ebbing away.

I was afraid that I was no longer a desirable woman. I was afraid to undress in front of him. My body carried the wrinkles, bumps, and sags of life's experiences. I was afraid he would tire of me and look to a younger woman with an hour-glass figure and smooth, creamy skin.

For eight months, we tumbled in the ecstasy of wild passion. It was wonderfully healing. The moment he stepped in the door, our energies collided and the woman in me rose up. Like two snakes, our bodies coiled around each other.

We had both felt the grief of separation.

I was ready to step right in again and allow the passion to consume me. I held that love so tightly in my arms, I squashed it! My lover began to feel suffocated. And I began to feel desperate, lost, and rejected as I felt him slip away from my grasp.

And so again I was to learn about another layer to those words: "unconditional love!"

The quickest way to lose love is to demand it. In my need to be loved again, to feel the joy and wonder of that magnificent sensual/sexual energy flowing through me, I killed the relationship by applying pressure through fear.

It was a timely reminder: that which you put out is what you get back. I feared losing him, and so I did.

There was no commitment. It had never been promised, and I knew that to be the case. I also knew that there were differences in our philosophy on life that would have lead to some interesting discussions without resolution. But my need to be held and loved was clouding my insight and perception. It was a selfish place I had entered, filled with hungry desire and longing.

Again I was being taught that no one else can fill the emptiness or erase the loneliness. Only love for self, from within that divine spiritual centre of one's being, can eradicate the loneliness and fill the emptiness with light.

When I let go of my lover, he returned, not as a lover but as a dear and beautiful friend. In this friendship is a love far richer and more beautiful than what had been. He gave me a magnificent gift: he helped me to find the woman in me. He helped me to discover and enjoy my sensuality and sexuality. He breathed life back into my body.

MY FRIEND

I fell in love with him the first moment I saw him. It was like reconnecting with someone I had known before, someone I had loved before. And so the greater test was upon me, for this love was not returned.

Months passed. In the silence of my heart, I cried. I fought the ache that lingered, secretly filling the spaces within. I held back that which I longed to give, knowing it would not be taken.

I watched him as he loved another, and I felt the beauty of their loving. I saw their smiles, their playful touches, the trust he placed in her keeping. I saw the laughter in their eyes.

This, then, is the greatest test of unconditional love: to love someone so much that you are willing to let go of them, to encourage them to love another with your blessing, for their highest good and full attainment of love.

Perhaps with time, the flames of love burning within me would drop to gentle embers. I could not un-love him. When he was near me, the moon goddess shone with her gentle and tender light. But when the other woman was close to him, she was as the sun in the high noon sky!

I loved these five men, but my friend was the one to whom I could say, "I loved you enough to let you love another. I loved you enough to allow you the joy of being in her arms. I loved you enough to want only that which is for your highest good. I loved you enough to love you unconditionally."

These five men have taught me:

1. to love without judging their behaviour and without seeking their approval;
2. to love people for exactly who they are in any given moment, without wanting to change them;

3. to love people in their deepest, darkest moments by stepping away from the drama, by putting self aside to fully understand the anguish within them, and to love from a place of compassion;
4. to love people without seeking love's return, without being in a place of fearing the loss of that love, and being in a place of self-love; and
5. to love people so deeply you are willing to let go of them for their highest good, allowing them to love another.

When we begin to love unconditionally, wars will end. Fear and greed, the hunger to be "in control" because of our insecurities, and the desire to be all powerful will disappear. When we learn to be powerful beings from a place of love instead of a place of fear, then our relationships with others will become joyful experiences. When we learn to love self, our love for others will expand, grow, and deepen because we will be in touch with who we truly are: beautiful and magnificent beings, the gods/goddesses within. And we will recognise the beauty in others.

That which you give out is that which you receive! If we are judgemental, we will be judged. If we wish to use our power to control others, we will be controlled. If anger fills our hearts and minds, anger will be directed back to us. If we allow ourselves to be depressed, we will draw depressed people to us. If we fear not being loved, we will struggle to be loved. If we believe we don't deserve to be loved, love will not come to us. If we fear success, success will not be ours to know.

But when we learn to love unconditionally, then we will be loved unconditionally. Perhaps the end of wars and tyranny, the end of greed and hatred, the end of imbalances in all areas of life begin with us learning to truly understand what *unconditional love* really means.

19 *Past Lives*

PAST LIVES CAN HAVE an effect on our present life. For those who may be sceptical about the existence of past lives, I recommend you read Dr Brian Weiss's book *Many Lives, Many Masters*. This book is based on the story of one of his patients, who turned Brian around from being an atheist to the amazing man he is today, addressing thousands of people all over the world on the effects of past lives.

There is a part of us that never dies. Call it what you will: the soul, the spirit, the subconscious, the super-conscious. It matters not what name you give it. Within that part of us is an amazing computer that has a memory bank far greater than any laptop or supercomputer. Within that memory bank are the memories of all our past lives. The World Wide Web is nothing compared to what each of us has stored away within this memory bank. For centuries, as our soul journeys through each successive life on this planet and in other realms, it has been methodically filing away the memories of those life times. All we have to do is go online, click on recall, and up comes a lifetime for us.

Mostly, we return for yet another life on this planet to heal the trauma of past lives, and to learn new and valuable lessons so that our soul may continue to grow and expand, evolving into its magnificence. As each human being evolves, the species as a whole evolves.

It is not always necessary to recall those lifetimes so that we may heal. Occasionally, it helps us to understand why certain patterns are present in this lifetime, and why we react to certain situations without understanding why. Often, emotions like anger and conditions like depression and self-sabotage have their roots in a past life. Past lives are not to be used as excuses; they are a base for understanding, growth, and healing.

There is no timeline for the return of the soul. I hear people say that the soul does not return under hundred years. The soul is not limited by time. It has been my experience [both personally and with my clients], I have encountered souls who have returned within two to three years of having died. There is a "quickening" within the realm of spirit; journeys are speeding up. The slower pace of 200 years ago no longer exists. People are returning quickly to speed up the evolution of their soul.

Not only do I believe souls are returning quickly to experience another lifetime, I believe also that many of us have chosen to experience several lifetimes within one life. I am quite certain that I have chosen that road. I can divide my life into five definite segments, each segment vastly different to the others, and each one has taught me more about myself, helping me to expand and grow in ways I would not otherwise have done.

There are recorded cases of young children having clear memories of their immediate past life. They have been able to give details of such things as the name of their street, a description of the house, where their school was, where the factories and shops were located, and the names of people they knew. Their accounts have proven to be accurate, even though in this life they have never visited the area and they live in a completely different part of the country.

Such a case came to my attention:

I was called to visit a lovely young mother who was having huge problems with her three year old son. For the child's father, it was a second marriage. In the father's previous marriage there had been three children. Two of the children and their mother had died in an accident. Dad had remarried, and they had a son of their own. This son would wake in the early hours of morning and chat to people in spirit. The talking would go on for about three hours. After these talks [which become very tiring and difficult for Mother and Father, interrupting their sleep], the child would then relate back to them details of the accident. The mother and father had never spoken to this child about the accident. At times, he spoke in a language far more advanced than that which would be expected of a three-year-old, more advanced than his normal conversations. Much of this was said in exactly the same way and with the same physical expressions as one of the older children who had died.

His conversations become more frequent, with accurate accounts of the accident. The mother has come to believe that her three-year-old son was an incarnation of a child from her husband's first marriage. I believe she was right. It was quite distressing for the child to have such memories. It was very distressing for the parents to have to work with their little one to bring balance and harmony back into their lives. As the child grows older the memories will fade, but for now it was distressing for all three of them. For father and son, night after night, the memory of the accident was kept alive. For the mother, there was the constant grief her husband was experiencing and the constant reliving of the trauma for her son. At times she felt like an outsider in her own child's experience.

I could not erase the memories for their son but I was able to help the mother understand how important she is in her child's life. She also had her feelings of what was happening acknowledged as the truth. With that acknowledgement came inner peace, the strength to speak more openly with her husband and the courage to help her son move beyond those memories.

Before you open a door to a former life, make sure it is in your best interest to do so. Curiosity and intrigue are not good enough reasons to go delving into ancient memory. Past-life recall is not a game; it can be a painful experience. There are no brownie points for having lived the life of a great ruler or scientist or artist. We have all had amazing lives, and we all have had lives we would rather not know about. You may see something you do not wish to see and that serves no purpose for you at this time.

Past-life recall is a way to heal something in this lifetime that you have brought through with you, a way to help your soul become more whole and beautiful than it already is. You may have had a previous life in which you were a thief and the lesson for you in this life is to be generous in sharing with others. You may have been a servant and in this life you need to learn how to be a leader. Perhaps in a previous life you were down trodden; the bully at work in your current life maybe there to teach you to stand up for yourself.

Most people have carried baggage with them into this life from a previous life. If you decide to explore a past-life with the intent of healing something in this lifetime, make sure you have a practitioner who can help you see the connections; someone who can support you as you integrate the lessons you need to learn from the memories of that past life.

20 *Freedom Or Release?*

FROM MY OWN LIFE experience, I have concluded that freedom is not about our outer world but rather an inner experience with self. When we see freedom as a goal, we are constantly putting it out there in front of us. Freedom then becomes elusive, always just out of reach. When we see it as a fulfilment, then it comes from a place of neediness.

I have seen wealthy people imprisoned by their wealth, and I have seen wealthy people living a joyful life of being free within their selves. I have seen people imprisoned by their poverty, whilst others, in the most horrific state of poverty, choose to use it to free themselves from the bondage of material possessions, to seek a deeper spiritual meaning to their life. And then there are those in between, who are either contented with what they have or, because of the inner hunger for freedom, strive to gather more money and more possessions. For them, enough is never enough.

I have heard people talk of wanting their freedom when they let go of a relationship, only to find that to walk alone brings a deep loneliness, an emptiness into their hearts. I have also spoken to people who have found a sense of freedom within a difficult relationship.

It is easy to blame others or the world around us for feeling trapped, lost, lonely, abandoned, afraid, overwhelmed by problems, and caught up in a whole bunch of negative feelings and experiences. I have been down that road many times. However, the older I get the freer I become, but not because of material possessions or because my experiences have become more mellow. When I filed for divorce, did that set me free? No. It released me from a relationship that no longer benefited either of us, but that is not freedom.

So what is freedom? I actually think the answer is simple, the truth is simple, but the achievement of it is perhaps one of the most difficult of all our experiences.

In asking the question, I went to Kahlil Gibran's book, *The Prophet*, to his chapter on freedom; as always, his beautiful thoughts set my mind to thinking. He wrote that you only gain freedom, *"...when you cease to speak of freedom as a goal and a fulfilment."*

His words softly settled in my mind. It is not about our outer experiences with the world, possessions, or people. Freedom comes when we begin to accept and love ourselves enough to want to fully stand in what is true for us; as Kahlil says further on in the same chapter, *"...when you rise up above these things naked and unbound."* Lack of difficulties does not bring freedom. Rising above the difficulties, finding our deep inner strength and courage, being true to self, loving self, it is these that bring freedom in our lives.

Money and worldly possessions cannot set us free. They can help us to enjoy our life, they can release us from debt and poverty, but they cannot give us freedom. People can release us from relationships, but they cannot give us our freedom. Freedom only comes when you begin to honour your soul's destiny, when you begin the process of loving self, when you choose to be in a place of happiness instead of pain and depression, when you find the strength and courage to become the beautiful and dynamic being you were created to be. No one can give that to you. That is a choice you need to make for yourself. We either choose to be in bondage or we choose to *"...rise above these things naked and unbound."* We choose to be free!

21 $\mathcal{D}$reams $\mathcal{O}$r $\mathcal{V}$isions?

I **HAVE BEEN FASCINATED** by dreams now for many years. I have studied and analysed both my own dreams and the dreams of other people. I have come to understand that our dreams fall into six different categories:

1. Ramblings of the mind: usually associated with confusion and fear, or simply a dumping of the hundreds of thoughts that plagued our mind throughout our busy day.
2. Events with our current life: what is happening in our workplace or personal life.
3. A visitation from someone in spirit.
4. Messages from our loved ones or guides to help us see what we need to see for the greater good of our life.
5. Prophecy: seeing into the future.
6. A replay of a past life.

I prefer to call the last four types of dreams "visions," for they are more than just the workings of our mind. They infer an interaction between self and someone else. There are several books out now on dream interpretation. The one I found to be the most accurate is Denise Linn's book, *The Hidden Power of Dreams*. So let's investigate these different types of dreams one at a time to see if they give clarity and understanding in what our dreams might mean for us.

RAMBLINGS OF THE MIND

These are usually dreams that you do not remember. There may be a vague understanding that you have just been dreaming a whole heap of images that make no sense. People who study dreams will tell you these types of dreams are a clearing of the built-up tension within the mind. They are usually present when we are going through a time of confusion, grief, fear, or any other negative experience. If you like, it is the mind's way of putting out the rubbish bins to be emptied; some of it will be gotten rid of, and some will be recycled.

If you are experiencing nights where you wake from these types of dreams feeling disturbed and restless, it may help to do a meditation of some kind, emptying the mind of its clutter and come into a place of stillness and peace. Other ways to help get rid of the clutter in the mind are to go for a long walk, ride a bike, do a workout at a gym, sit by the sea or under a tree, or talk to someone who is a good listener. Keep trying until you find some way that helps to empty the turmoil of the day from your mind.

EVENTS WITHIN OUR LIFE

These dreams are often present when something of significance is happening in our life: events such as a change in employment, moving to a new home, becoming a parent or grandparent, going for a holiday, having relationship problems, children leaving home, drug or alcohol abuse, or the death of a loved one.

Usually it is easy for us to see the link between the dream and the event. Sometimes, these dreams can be unpleasant, but this does not necessarily mean that the dream will come true. More often than not, what is happening in the dream is a reflection of our fear that something will go wrong; conversely, it may reflect our hopes and positive feeling that all will be well.

Here is an example of such a dream: Your daughter may be pregnant and you may dream that she will miscarry. It is not to say that because you have dreamt it, your daughter will miscarry; it is more likely that this fear is playing out in your mind. If you (or your mother) have miscarried, the fear is very present for you. The dream may be present as a message to help you acknowledge your fear and find a way to come into a place of peace and harmony.

A VISITATION FROM SOMEONE WHO HAS DIED

In my work as a grief counsellor, I often hear, "I would love to have a sign from my loved one that they are with me." Then five minutes later they will say, "I dreamt about them the other night. It was so clear I could have sworn they were here with me."

Dreams are the easiest way that our loved ones can connect with us after they have passed into spirit. We are often so engrossed in our pain, our grief, we fail to realise what an enormous effort it takes for our loved ones in spirit to make contact with us.

If you dream of your loved one who has passed over, please don't dismiss it as just a dream. Your loved one has worked hard to come through to you, and your Delta state of unconsciousness (or no consciousness) is the best way they can reach out to you, through your dreams. Take note of how they look and what they are trying to say to you; and trust that this is real, that this person is in contact with you through your dreams.

Here is a good example of a dream one of my clients experienced. Her husband had died two years prior to her having this dream.

Helen and Russel had been Cub Scout leaders. In her dream, they had taken a group of Cub Scouts into the city of Melbourne for a day outing. Helen became aware that Russel had taken half the group and got on a tram. He had left Helen alone with the rest of the group. Frustrated, she called out, "Where are we meant to meet? How do we catch up with each other?" At that point she awoke and heard the instruction to go and write. In her dazed state, she got a pen and pad. Without thinking, she began to write as Russel spoke to her. Later, after she had further sleep, she read what had been written:

- *I am only a tram stop away.*
- *There is a set timetable for everyone.*
- *In bold capitals she had written "DO NOT CATCH AN EARLY TRAM."*
- *Fully enjoy the tram stop where you are now.*
- *Know that when your time comes I will be at the next tram stop waiting for you.*
- *And again in bold lettering, "NO STRESS!"*

This amazing combination of dream and instructed writing gave Helen a deep feeling of peace and strength to move on in her life. It helped her to let go of Russel and to move forward, creating a new life. The message is clear. Helen is not meant to join Russel yet. She still has a lot of living to do, and he was asking her to move forward and enjoy where she is right now.

MESSAGES FROM OUR LOVED ONES OR GUIDES

This is a little different to the previous type of vision. This is not so much about making the contact, but your guides are passing on to you messages from which you can learn and grow.

Sometimes, these images are quite beautiful, and at other times, they can be quite scary. If you have a dream that is intense and quite frightening in its imagery, it is rare that the images are meant as real life warnings. You need to take a deep breath, get up and make yourself a cup of tea or coffee, then sit quietly and analyse the dream. This is where a good dream interpretation book, such as Denise

Linn's book, comes in handy. More often than not, the apparent negative images have a strong and powerful message for you.

Here are some dream interpretation images that work for me; I only share them so you may begin to see such dreams in a different way. At the back of Denise's book, she has a comprehensive list if images that I find very accurate. However, we are all individuals, and one image may mean one thing for me and something quite different for you. The following list is just to get you started on thinking differently about disturbing dreams:

- Running water: is about emotions. If you are drowning in a fast-flowing river, it probably means you are allowing pain and grief, anger, or resentment to get the best of you; you are "drowning" in that emotion. If, on the other hand, you are floating on a fast-moving river, it probably means that you are in a joyful place and may be a little ungrounded in that joyfulness, such as a new romance.
- Still water: is about your spirituality. Diving deep into still water is a sign of saying you are on the right track with your spiritual journey and your spiritual growth will deepen. Drowning in still water may mean that you are not working on the spiritual aspect of your life enough, or it may mean that a change is coming where that which you have always believed may no longer serve you.
- Fire: You need to cleanse or getting rid of what no longer serves you.
- Car: You need to be in control of your life. You are the driver of your life. A crash may mean you have come to the end of this part of your life and a new part is about to begin. It does not necessarily mean you are going to be in a car accident. A new car would mean you have begun a new phase in your life.
- Bus or Train: Being in a bus or train crash may mean that certain people you have been travelling with in this lifetime

are about to leave. For me, trains and buses (as opposed to a single car) are about the people who are a part of my life: family, friends, work colleagues, and so on.

- Plane: If it is a good flight, it may be validation that you are flying high and well at this time in your life. A plane crash may be a warning for you to take time out for a holiday or you will "crash," or it may mean there is a change coming and this part of your flight is about to end.
- Birth of a baby: Usually means new beginnings.
- An artist: You need to be creative in your life.
- An Earthquake: You have become stagnant and your life needs a bit of a shake up.
- A tsunami: Like fire, cleansing out that which no longer serves you.
- A volcano: Something in your life is about to explode; it may even be you if you don't take the pressure off yourself.

We can learn much from these types of visions that our guides and loved ones can send us through our time of dreaming. It pays to keep a dream journal if you are experiencing a lot of these types of visions. Often there are connections or patterns to be seen as you look back over your dreams. One dream may only be a segment of the whole picture.

PROPHECY

The majority of my clients have dreams in the previous category. However, very occasionally I get a client who is a prophet; in other words, someone who can see into the future. This involves the workings of the right side of the brain, which is also where our dreams are created. Usually these people are aware of their psychic abilities. Their visions of the future are not limited to their dream world but are often experienced during the normal part of their daily activities. Therefore, when they have a dream that is of the future, they understand its content because, over and over, they have had proof that what they have dreamed has come true.

But prophecies are not certain to occur. Prophecies, especially those around negative events, are a warning that something needs to change in order to prevent this possible occurrence from happening. The long-term visions from the prophet Nostradamus were given to us as a warning to change our ways to prevent these events from occurring. His visions were saying to us, "If you stay on this destructive path, if you don't take heed of what we are saying, then this is what will happen."

Not all prophecies are of a negative nature; often it can be of beautiful things to come, such as someone having a baby.

The role of a prophet is a tough one. Most prophets are very quiet about what they see. They fear being ridiculed if they share their visions. They have to learn to trust what they see, and they often doubt their abilities. They don't always enjoy being prophets because of the sometimes disturbing visions that come to them. And when the visions come to them in the form of dreams, they have to learn the difference between a prophetic dream and one that simply holds a message for them.

If you are having prophetic dreams that come true, please do not blame yourself for the event happening. You are in no way making these things happen. You are simply a messenger from spirit, awakening people to the possibility of events occurring, hence giving people a chance to prevent that event from happening or giving them a chance to embrace it.

A REPLAY OF A PAST LIFE

The events and effects of a past life can find recognition and hopefully healing through our dreams. It is as though our soul knows what needs to be healed from a past life and prompts our memory bank to release the appropriate visions of the past for us to look at. Why? So that we can see fears we have brought into this lifetime or old patterns that need to change for our soul's advancement.

These past-life recalls, seen through our dreams, usually repeat themselves several times, the exact same dream over and over.

I experienced one such recall over a number of years. For about six years, I would have the exact same dream and wake up screaming at the exact same place in the dream: unable to go through a door ahead of me. I was unable to see the end of the dream but I knew it would not be a good outcome for me. It seemed I was avoiding, at a deep level of knowingness, facing the end result. There would be long spans of time without the dream, and then it would reappear, stronger than before.

In the dream, I was being held hostage and forced into a horrid room. I was a male about fourteen years old. The setting was in about the thirteenth or fourteenth century. A fourteen-year-old boy was a young man in those days. It came to a head when I was doing one of Doreen Virtue's courses and she guided us through a past-life recall meditation. As soon as I entered into the meditative state, the events of the dream came flooding back to me. This time, I suppose because I had the support of others around me, I was able to go through the door. What lay beyond the door was a body rack. The person operating the rack in that lifetime was my father in this lifetime. It was a form of torture and punishment where the body was stretched from both ends. It is excruciatingly painful and usually ends in death as the body is literally pulled apart. I never had the dream again.

From that recall came immense understanding as to why my father and I had struggled in this lifetime. We had fought against each other for centuries. Always it was a struggle for power, for domination over the other. Once seen, I then had the ability to let go of that struggle, bring in the healing we both so needed, and to begin the process of forgiveness, learning to respect each other and allowing our love to deepen.

If you are having a dream that keeps on repeating itself, there is a strong possibility your mind is releasing an old memory of a past life that needs you to take note. Try and get the message it is conveying to you. There is a reason why that same dream keeps coming back to you. Once the message is seen, the dream will leave you and you can step into the healing.

Our dreams are a very powerful part of our night time experiences. There is no such thing as "just a dream." Whether it is the release of tension, confusion, or fear though incoherent ramblings; an event from our current life; a visit from a deceased loved one; a message from our guides; a prophecy; or a past-life recall, our dreams can give us great insights into who we are and what we need to learn.

22 *Astral Travelling*

ASTRAL TRAVEL IS THAT state when our soul leaves our body and heads off to explore other places. I am often asked, "What is astral travel and how does it happen?" To understand astral travel we need to understand the different levels of consciousness that we move through in the course of a day.

There are four levels of consciousness:

- Beta: is that state when you are wide awake and talking, moving in a fully conscious and deliberate way.
- Alfa: is our daydreaming state and is the level of consciousness that most people go into when they are meditating.
- Theta: is that moment before sleep when you are still aware but only just aware. Some people can maintain this state in a deep meditation. This is the state that a lot of mediums are in when they are deliberately in contact with those who have died. It is the realm linking the conscious and unconscious mind, the world of spirit with the world of humanity; it is the twilight between day and night.
- Delta: is when you are sound asleep, your body is in a state of total unconsciousness. However, in this Delta state, your mind and soul are free to roam.

It is in this Delta state that most people are free to do their astral travelling. The majority of us are unaware of the journeys we take during our astral travels.

As a nurse, I have known patients who have been unconscious due to illness, or during an operation, describe to me everything that happened during those periods. They observed their own body and procedures that nurses and doctors carried out to help in their healing. Their souls were often floating close to the ceiling of the room or standing beside the medical team.

It is also when we are in this state that those in spirit can contact us easily, for in truth we are in the same place of spirit as they, when our physical bodies are no longer able to be interactive.

23 *Self-Love And Forgiveness*

MY HEART ACHED AS I listened to Don's story. Don was in his mid-fifties. He sat opposite me, a tight ball of tension, his energy field was depleted to a level where he could become ill. He spoke bluntly and honestly about his life. He held nothing back.

Don worked long hours, six to seven days a week. He owned a business that was running at less than 50 percent capacity. He allowed no time for pleasurable activities. He had no reserves of energy and no enthusiasm for his work or any other part of his life. Bogged down in a mire of debt and responsibility, Don could not see his way forward. Along with his business, his inner core was dying.

Don was caught up in the ugly, crushing net of responsibility. Each day, that net wrapped itself around him more tightly than the day before. He would feel guilty if he took time off from work, being for ever mindful of the downward run of his business. What he could not see was that, at least in part, his business was crumbling because he was crumbling. Don could not see that because he was low in energy, was extremely tired, and therefore irritable; this was conveyed to his employees, who also lost enthusiasm for the work.

He had described symptoms he was experiencing in his body: high blood pressure, irritable bowel syndrome, and chest pains due to stress. Don was also unable to sit still for any period of time. Here was a man well on the way to creating a serious illness of some kind. The enormous pressure he had put himself under, both at work and in his personal life, was bringing him down. His body was screaming at him, "Stop, for God sake, stop!"

I looked him directly in the eyes and said, "If you do not begin to honour and respect and love yourself enough to take time out from this awful mess, time to be still and listen to your heart instead of you head, you will not be here to sort the mess out. Someone else will have to do it for you, because you will be in a coffin."

"Love myself?" He replied. "What is that like? I have never been loved. I have had my physical and mental needs cared for, but love? I don't even know what that is, what that word means!"

I asked him, "What makes your heart sing?"

His answer was like a knife thrust into my guts: "What makes my heart sing? I have no idea. I don't think my heart has ever sung. What is it like to have your heart sing?"

I am often asked: how does one love self?

Don began with little steps. His first step was to honour the precious life he has been given. He resolved to take one day off from work each week: a day to be still and to listen to his heart beat, his breath moving in and out of his body. He needed time to relax and redirect his thoughts away from all the stress and the anxiety of his work-related problems. We all need time out from the constant pressure of life simply to be, to do only those things that give us pleasure. Having fun is so important. What feeds the soul and feeds our energy is relaxation, laughter, and allowing ourselves to do things that make our heart sing.

Don's second step was to practice forgiveness of others and of self. Forgiveness is not about making what has happened, what created the pain and separation, okay. It is about stepping away from being a victim. He could go on being bitter and angry, or he could set his self free from that entanglement.

Bitterness and anger at others do not actually affect others anywhere near as much as they affect self. Forgiveness is not about being a good and spiritual person and doing what is right. His forgiveness was not so much about letting go of the negative thoughts and feelings around what had been said or done to him. It was about not allowing what had happened to label who he was. Forgiveness is about not allowing self to sit in the wretchedness of the past. It's about choosing to step into healing and happiness.

Don's third step was to work on respect for self. If he does not respect his own life, how can he expect others to respect who he was and what he did? So how could he gain self-respect? He began removing from his life those things that he knew were not good for him:

- Bad eating habits
- Guilt
- Negative relationships that pulled him down and helped to destroy his self-esteem

Together we explored taking from his life things that did not help him to feel good about himself:

- Anger
- Resentment
- Cigarettes
- Anything of a negative nature

Then we looked to see what we could replace those things with:

- A more positive attitude
- The desire to be healthy and to be at peace and in harmony with self and the world around him.

The moment Don began to make a stand for self by removing those things within his life that did not nurture him, he will begin to feel the first hint of warmth towards self, to feel good for being strong and having the courage to say no to those things and to those people who diminish him.

What naturally follows on from forgiveness and self-respect is self-love; that little thought that begins with: *Well, maybe I am an okay kind of person. You know, I am rather good at doing this and that, and, actually, I have a lot going for me when I really look at myself, when I am honest about the lovely part of me.* What began for Don [and can for us] with those realisations were the first sparks of self-love, the first steps into healing a low self-esteem.

No one else can give that to us or do it for us. Creating self-love is an inner journey, the struggle between our heart and our mind, getting rid of the inner critic with its constant barrage of negative thoughts and stepping into the honesty of our beautiful self. It is a bit like a TV program with homes that are so full of junk no one can actually find anything or move with any freedom. When, like my client, we fill our mind with negative thoughts, they begin to pile up until we can no longer see the beautiful room that is our heart and soul. We lose our freedom, and every move we make only adds to the pile of junk. Don had to start by getting rid of the junk in his mind.

That is where Don had gotten to in his life. His head was so full of negative junk, he then went on to create that junk in his outer world. When I began to feed back to him the beauty within him, tears welled up in this hardened business man's eyes. His masculine side fought hard to stop them from falling, and then it all got too much and fall they did. I believe that it was one of the few times he had allowed himself to be vulnerable. I felt privileged that he felt safe enough to cry. Perhaps for the first time, he was allowing himself to be honest with who he truly was: a beautiful and loving man.

Don reminded me of a tiny bird inside an egg shell, all cramped up but struggling to break free. All of a sudden, he began to peck away at the shell, and suddenly the shell gave way and he found himself taking his first deep breath of freedom.

Self-love is a beautiful experience. Self-love is not of the ego but of the heart. It does not make us feel we are better than others. Self-love, self-acceptance, and acknowledgement of our own inner beauty allow us to see the inner beauty in others; allow us to feel the oneness with all of life and to understand how very precious this experience called "life" is. Then we begin to create in our outer world what is happening for us in our inner world.

People will respect us more because we have learned to respect ourselves. People will love us more because we have learned to love ourselves. The clutter in the outer world will begin to diminish because we have gotten rid of the rubbish from our inner world.

Bit by bit, Don cut away at the crushing net that had so entangled him. His life began to flow freely and he began to feel the first signs of joyfulness pulsating through him. What began to happen for my client was a miracle. We, too, can create that miracle. Really, what have we got to lose? Just a whole bunch of garbage!

24 *Compromise*

FOR MOST OF MY life, I have struggled with finding a healthy balance between doing what is right for me and, at the same time, having consideration for others' beliefs and welfare.

Compromise has both a positive and a negative side to it.

When we compromise in a negative way, usually for the sake of keeping the peace, it creates a niggling feeling of resentment that usually smoulders into anger. It reads rather like,   "I gave up this part of my life because you didn't like it." Or "I compromised and did this other thing instead, and I have always resented having to do so." It creates in us a festering of unspoken negative thoughts that spread their poison to our hearts.

At the age of seven, I became aware of my psychic abilities. I had no name for them; I just knew I could see people in spirit and chat to them. Back then there was no support or explanation. Psychics were considered unbalanced. My father told me it was naughty and the workings of dark forces, that I must stop it. But a question remained with me, until I found the courage at fifty-four to allow myself to be who I came here to be: a psychic medium. The question was, if this is the work of dark forces, then how come it is so beautiful? Even at that young age, I knew my father was wrong. But the result of that threat in my father's voice was many years of living with the fear of non-acceptance, of compromising my soul and the work I came here to do.

My first husband feared the gift and felt challenged by it; Jeff, my second husband, told me it was all garbage and didn't want to talk about it. With each husband, I compromised for the sake of peace. But was I at peace? No. Underneath, the resentment simmered. I could not be who I wanted to be. A part of me was not accepted. I allowed myself to become who they wanted me to be.

When Jeff died, I chose never to allow my soul to be compromised again. I found the courage to say, "Never again will I hide who I am to make other people accept me and feel comfortable with me." Members of my family have been challenged by my stance. I lost many friends, but what I gained was self-acceptance, self-respect, and self-love. I also gained a whole bunch of new friends; the most beautiful people I could hope to have. Whatever I had lost by standing in my truth and not compromising my own self, by allowing myself to be the individual I came here to be, was far outweighed by what I had gained.

This kind of negative compromise, because we are afraid to stand up for what is true and real for us, brings about a sense of defeat and low self-esteem. It eats at the very core of us. We may feel we are compromising to keep the peace in a situation, but the real compromise that is happening is not in the outer situation but within us. Out of fear of the consequences of standing in our truth, we compromise our very essence and therefore inhibit our soul's growth.

The positive side of compromise is about respecting those we love. It is about allowing self to be an individual, but it is also about allowing others their right to be individuals.

This is how I see it: we are all nourished by the same master chef, from the same divine oven. But we are individuals; you may not like pumpkin and I may not like peas. The plate that is placed before us as we sit at the table of life may be very different. Does it matter? We can still sit at the same table and share our pleasure in being nourished, even if we do it differently.

All it would have taken for Jeff and I to feel more comfortable with our individual concepts of psychic ability would have been for him to acceptance my feelings and show respect for our differing understanding. I could have quietly used my abilities to help other people without involving Jeff. And my lovely husband would have allowed me to use my abilities without ridiculing me. It was Jeff's right not to believe in what I do. It was my right to embrace it. The negative compromise, of never speaking to each other about my psychic abilities, created resentment and anger in me because I could not be true to myself.

If Jeff and I had been able to step into a positive compromise, then neither of us would have suffered. We would have remained our own beautiful individual selves, and we would have both overcome our fears. Jeff would have overcome his fear of my psychic ability and his fear of life beyond death. I would have overcome my fear of not being accepted and loved. If you are in a relationship with someone who finds a part of your life difficult, or you find something they enjoy doing difficult, then seek out a positive compromise that does not diminish either of you. As Kahlil Gibran, that beautiful author of *The Prophet*, wrote, "Fill each other's cup but drink not from one cup."

Interestingly, after he passed through that flimsy curtain of death, Jeff became my greatest ally and help in my psychic journey. He came through another medium [who knew nothing about me] and told me that all I had tried to convey to him was true. It took his death for us to truly find each other and sit at the same table of life.

The life Jeff and I had together was beautiful; we had an amazing experience, but how much more rewarding and beautiful it would have been if we both had allowed the positive side of compromise to be present in our relationship. That which was not to be spoken of, my psychic ability, became the only barrier between us, a barrier that need not have existed.

On the other side of the balance, being too demanding of your rights can be just as destructive an experience as being too compromising. This also comes out of fear rather than love and acceptance. It's the attitude of "I will be who I want to be and do what I want to do and I will crush anyone who gets in my way."

This attitude lacks compassion, is not of spirit, and may prevent you from serving your fellow human beings. Therefore, it does nothing for the growth of your heart, mind, and soul. The fear on which this attitude is based is usually the fear of being less than others. From that root of fear grows the tree of greed. It is not necessarily a greed for material possessions, but perhaps more so a greed for power. It is a heartless and unhealthy way of standing your ground. A negative attitude creates a negative outcome. You may achieve what you want to achieve, but how many people will love and respect you? You may get what you want, but at the very core of your being is loneliness and isolation.

So how do we become strong individuals? As with all things pertaining to a successful life, it begins with loving self and respecting ourselves enough to stand up for our beliefs and heart longings, to want to develop all of our potential. This does not come at the cost of others, but rather includes others.

That which you believe you create; that which you sow you reap; that which you put out comes back to you. Say it in as many ways as you want to, but in the end it is the same ancient law of attraction. When I decided to let go of fear, to stand up for my beliefs and respect myself, I drew to myself beautiful new friends from whom I gained respect.

When we step into allowing self to expand, grow, and become a beautiful and strong individual, then we draw to us people of a like mind. These people then become our support, and we become their support. Together we grow. Together we eat at the same table of life.

You still may not like pumpkin, and I may still not like peas, but does it matter?

25 *Guilt And Resentment*

WHAT PURPOSE DOES GUILT and resentment play in our life? Even the sound of those two words has a heavy feeling. Say them in your mind a few times and feel the energy of the words; guilt, resentment, guilt, resentment, guilt, resentment. They immediately bring our energy levels down. Do we need to live with those heavy energies?

I have come to the conclusion that neither is helpful in any way. Both are a waste of beautiful energy and time.

Resentment

I participated in a workshop designed to help business managers. The facilitator, wrote on his white board a simple saying I now use all the time in all areas of my life:

If something is not working for you, you have one of three options:

- *Put up with it,*
- *Change it, or*
- *Get out of it.*

Resentment fills our hearts and minds when we are unwilling to change the situation or walk away from it. Resentment comes from putting up with it. So does that make it the other person's problem?

From my own personal experience, I would have to say no. I am the one who is either creating this problem or allowing it to exist. I was resentful and angry when I stopped living my own truth out of fear of not being accepted and loved. So to whom was I really resentful? It wasn't Jeff or anyone else. I was resentful and angry towards myself for not having the courage and strength to stand up for myself.

We tend to lay the blame for our resentment at the feet of others:

- "You made me do it."
- "I only did this because I knew it was what you wanted me to do."
- "I didn't do this because I knew you didn't want me to do it."
- "I am always doing everything for everyone else, but who ever does anything for me?"
- "Why should I have to carry this burden? It's not my problem."

And so on. Does this ring a bell?

Resentment often comes with what we imagine to be true:

- Often what we imagine comes through our negative thoughts and is probably based on how we feel about ourselves.
- Sometimes it comes from our interpretation of events.
- And then there is that which I call the ultimate truth, the truth that comes when we can be deeply honest with ourselves, stripping back our hidden agendas and laying bare the simple truth.

When Jeff died, I experienced the different layers of reactions before I was able to admit to the real truth of what his death meant for me.

- My first reaction was *I am devastated. I can't go on. I just want to die too.*
- Weeks later I stepped into the second stage: *Life is bloody tough but in truth, I am coping.*

- And then many months later came the ultimate truth in the third stage of grief. One of the greatest gifts my darling man gave me was to die. Through his death, I was released to become the person I am today; not the housewife I was, but the healer and teacher I came here to be. Through my one-on-one work as a counsellor and medium, through my books and through my workshops, I have allowed myself to step into my soul's purpose.

Sadly, none of this would have happened if Jeff had not died.

Let's say you have just been fired from a job or your relationship with your partner has just ended. What is the truth in this for you? Where are you going with your thoughts?

- Are you in your imagined truth? *They don't like me at work. I always knew the boss had it in for me. I bet my partner is having an affair and that is why this has come to an end. He [or she] doesn't think I am good enough.* Are you sitting in resentment?
- Or are you in the truth of the result of an event? *Yes, well, I knew that people were going to be put off, and I suspected I was going to be made redundant. Yes, well, I have known for some time this marriage was going to come to an end. We were just not meant to be together. It hurts, but in a way I am relieved it is over.*
- Or are you in you're the ultimate truth? *This redundancy now gives me a chance to seek out doing something different with my life. The break-up in this relationship now gives me the chance to fully explore who I am and how I want my personal life to be.*

It is a process to discover the hidden and ultimate truth. The first reaction pulls you down, places you fully in the stream of resentment, and diminishes you. The second leaves you in no-man's land. The third truth releases you to do things differently and allows you to become excited about your life once again.

In order to release resentment and come into a place of healing, I believe we need to be deeply honest with our selves. When we look beneath the resentment, we will usually find either this is how we feel about ourselves or there is some fear we need to face. Once we see the fear, we then need to ask the questions: "How am I relating to this fear? How did this fear originate? What can I do to change this situation? How can I gather the strength and courage I need to stand in my truth?" And the final question: "Do I want to change this situation or am I actually enjoying being angry and resentful?"

There is a certain power in being angry and resentful. But does that power help us to grow and expand into the beautiful being our soul wants us to be? Anger and resentment have their place, but if we continually sit in those feelings, ultimately we will be hurt by them. People are drawn to eyes that sparkle and smile. People walk away from eyes that show resentment and anger. They will become frustrated or bored by us or, worse, fearful of us. Being continuously resentful creates a lonely existence.

When resentment and anger are present, they are a signal to look deeper at a situation, to challenge our place in that situation, and to allow us the chance to change it or walk away from it. That choice is entirely ours; no one else can make that decision for us.

Guilt

So many clients walk into my consultation room carrying the heavy burden of guilt. Each time I see this, I feel sad because I have "been there and done that." I understand how draining and totally unnecessary this state of guilt is. That is not to say we should not be responsible for what we say and do. Of course we need to learn from our mistakes. But to remain in a place of self-recrimination is a form of self-punishment that serves no purpose.

When I have sat in guilt, I have sensed my soul give a big sigh and say, "Okay, time to move on now. Are we finished with this guilt? No? Oh, how much more time do you have to wait before you decide to stop punishing yourself so we [my soul and I] can get back to being light-hearted and beautiful?"

Really, when we look at the situation we are feeling guilty about, does the guilt change anything? No, and that is the point of it all: guilt is pointless! To make this situation better within self, we need to start being honest about what has taken place, taking steps towards healing it, and tossing out the guilt.

If there is something in your life that has created feelings of guilt, perhaps you need to see the lesson in that situation then forgive self for whatever wrong you feel you have done. When we let go of the guilt and allow ourselves to love self, then the healing can begin.

Guilt and resentment imprison us. Honesty and healing set us free.

After a period of struggling with resentment, during a precious moment of insight, I wrote the following poem:

> *To only see darkness*
> *Is a reflection*
> *Of one's inner self.*
>
> *Always there is*
> *A guiding light if we*
> *Allow ourselves to see it.*
>
> *The choice is ours,*
> *To sit in the darkness*
> *Or walk in the light.*

26 *What Is Silence?*

DEPENDING ON HOW WE are feeling, silence is either welcomed or feared. The constant busyness of our modern society allows us to dodge being still in silence. Yet, to be still in silence is one of the most powerful experiences we can have. When we are still in silence, there is only one way for us to go; back to our soul. Native Americans go on a vision quest; Australian Aboriginal people go on walkabouts; some people do month-long silent retreats. They are all seeking the hidden treasures in silence. Buddha did it for forty days and forty nights, sitting under a tree. Jesus did it for forty days and forty nights, sitting out in the desert. Both of these masters came into enlightenment because of their experience with silence. Both faced their inner demons, their negative thoughts and feelings, until they came face to face with their beauty, their divinity, and their total love for self and all that is.

This is how my dictionary defines "silence":

- Absence of any sound or noise, stillness
- The fact or state of being silent, muteness
- Omission of mention, to pass over a matter in silence
- Oblivion
- Secrecy
- To put or bring to silence
- To put to rest [doubts etc.], quiet

Poets and philosophers throughout the centuries have tried to capture the essence of silence. We can't because, as the dictionary indicates, there are so many layers to silence.

The silence I write about here is the inner silence that brings total peace to the mind and heart. It is the silence that can exist in the midst of outer turmoil. It is the silence that allows the restless mind to be quieted and find clarity; that allows the heart to beat at a gentle and slower pace. It is the silence that helps us to find that bottomless well of strength. It is that place that, like a rainbow bridge, spans the space between our humanity and our divinity.

Meditation

This is perhaps one of the hardest meditations to do. Don't become disheartened if you don't master it right away. Practice makes perfect.

The first few times you do this meditation, you may find yourself having an inner fight with your thoughts. When thoughts appear, just recognize them and then let them go, continuously coming back into the meditation. It may help you to record your own voice and to play it each time you do this meditation. Recording the meditation may help to bring you back into it each time your thoughts try to take you away from the meditation.

Make sure you are in a quiet place where you will not be interrupted. Turn off your phones. If it is daytime, close the blinds and cocoon yourself in your room. If you like, light a candle. Make yourself comfortable. You can stretch out on the floor or bed, or sit comfortably in a chair. It is important for you to not be distracted by any bodily discomfort. Don't be tempted to use music, for it too will distract you from the aim of this meditation. You can also do this meditation outside in a natural setting, but you need to make sure nobody else is around to disturb you. It is a good one to do in your car by the sea or in a forest.

- *Close your eyes. Take a few deep breaths. With each inward breath, visualize yourself drawing in soft golden light. With each outward breath, release the tension in your body. Keep doing this, noting the rise and fall of your abdomen, until you feel that all tension has left your body. It may take a while so just enjoy feeling the tension leaving your body, the peace and quiet surrounding you.*

- *Now, turn your attention to the sounds outside your home or your car. Let go of all thought and just concentrate on the sounds. Don't label the sounds: there is a car, that's a bird singing and so on. Just be aware of the sounds. Give yourself a few minutes to simply experience the sounds of the outer world. Each time a thought comes, let go of it and return to listening to the sounds.*

- *Now turn you attention to the sounds within your home or car: the refrigerator humming, the creak of a roof, the tick of a clock. Again, when the thoughts threaten to enter, return to concentrating on the sounds.*

- *Now turn your attention to the sounds within you: your breath, swallowing, ringing in your ears. Simply listen without comment, without the need to change anything. Again, if thoughts sneak in simply dismiss them.*

- *You are beginning to move into the core centre of your being.*

- *Visualize yourself at the top of a very long but sturdy ladder. This ladder leads down into a deep ravine. The cliff is a sheer drop to the bottom. There are forty rungs to this ladder. Begin counting at forty and go down the ladder a rung at a time until you have reached rung number one.*

- *You are now in a deep, deep place where there is total silence. Step off the last rung into the ravine. Sit cross legged on the floor of the ravine. From way up above you, a shaft of pure golden light streams down into the ravine. It falls onto your shoulders and down to the ground. You sit in total silence, encapsulated in this beam of golden light.*

- *Your body begins to change. It dissolves into a ball of deep pink light, a pink the colour of magenta, softly glowing yet bright and intense.*

There is only silence. In that silence, there is nothing but the golden light and you as you truly are, this beautiful and radiant soul of divine love. In this moment, this precious moment, you are one with and part of Great Spirit, and Great Spirit is one with and part of you. Within the golden light of spirit, you are enfolded in love so beautiful and pure that it makes your soul glow even brighter. This is you, this ball of rich deep pink. This is the energy, the essence of your divine self. This is who you truly are.

- *Allow yourself time to enjoy this moment, this very special moment.*
- *Gently, the beam of light retracts itself, and you find your body begins to reappear. The deep pink light remains, integrating itself into your body, integrating into every cell, every muscle.*
- *The ravine comes back into focus, and you see the ladder waiting to take you up and out of the ravine. Place your foot on the bottom rung and begin to climb, counting upwards from one to forty as you climb, rung by rung, back up to the top.*
- *Listen to the sounds within your room. Let the sounds of the outside world come to you. Wiggle your fingers and toes. Open your eyes.*

The more you master this meditation, the more you will feel the shift away from a tense and worried being to one who can be at peace in the midst of turmoil.

In the silence of our inner divine self, our soul self, there are oceans of love and strength, peace, and happiness.

After my mother died, she used to come through to me and say, "Remember who you are. Remember!" It took me a while before I understood what she meant. So I now pass her message on to you.

In the silence, the deep silence of the divine self, remember who you are. Remember!

27   *The Giant Within Us*

ONE OF THE GREATEST giants I have known was my mother. You may not have heard of Lillian Dunn, mother of six children, who died at age ninety-two after five operations for cancer and two major strokes. You now read of her amazing strength and courage to fight back and reclaim life. She struggled during World War 11, alone with four children, two of them deaf and all of them with measles; she was able to struggle on with hardly any sleep and near to collapsing from exhaustion. The stories of my mother's courage and strength are endless.

There is no one else who could have set a more solid foundation of strength for me. By her example, she helped me walk a turbulent path. My mother helped me to find the courage to go on when I felt diminished by my experiences. In her quiet way, tapping into her deep well of spirituality and hope, my mother found the giant within her. And all the while, through all of her hardships, my mother sang. And in those songs I have found the inner strength to walk with my own inner giant.

We all have a giant within us. You may not know you have an inner giant, but you do. We all have a choice; get to know our giant or remain small. Either way it is okay. It really doesn't matter, except if we decide to remain small, we will never know the joy of standing tall. But then, fear at times can be greater than the need to have a joyful life. When one learns to loves self, fear can always be overcome.

I have two DVD's in my library that I turn to when I feel the fever of the virus of smallness inside of me: *Conversations With God* – the story of, Neale Donald Walsche, the author, and his experience of moving from poverty to success, and *The Peaceful Warrior* [based on the book of the same name], the true story of an American athlete with Olympic potential who fought back after a motorbike accident to reclaim the giant within him.

There are many stories throughout history of people who fought against the odds to allow themselves to honour and claim the giant within them. We don't have to become a Nelson Mandela, Martin Luther King, Louise Hay, Denise Linn or Neale Donald Walsche. It may not be our path in this life time. But that does not mean we cannot be giants.

Your giant may be a peaceful warrior. Your giant may not have a public voice, but can change the lives of others by setting an example, as my mother did. Your giant may need you to meditate, to go deeper into self, and find who you are. Your giant may be the teacher or healer in you, the artist, scientist, plumber, a handyman, or a wonderful parent.

Your giant is your soul; the eternal spirit within you, walking through centuries with Great Spirit; our connection to all of the cosmos; our inner god or goddess; the essence of who we truly are.

Believe it or not, you do have a giant within you. Take time to see who your giant is and feel the joyfulness, the hope and strength that comes in discovering the magnificence of your own inner giant.

28 *Passion*

PASSION, REGARDLESS OF WHAT that passion is for, involves our sexual/sensual energy. We have, for too long, separated out our sexual energy from the rest of us. It is not separate. How can it be? We were born with beautiful sexual energy that plays a vital part in our life, apart from the more obvious sexual encounters. It never leaves us. Sexual energy is perhaps one of the most misunderstood elements of our existence.

What is passion? The dictionary gives many meanings:

- Any kind of feeling or emotion especially of compelling force
- Sexual love
- An instance of experience
- Strong or extravagant fondness, enthusiasm, or desire for anything

My definition of passion is perhaps a little less conventional. For me, it is fire in the belly that breathes light, warmth and life into any situation.

Be it for sexual reasons, work, creativity, education, or any other aspect of our life, passion is a life force flowing through us. You can see that life force when you are with someone who is deeply passionate and committed to something in their life. Their energy shimmers. You can sense or feel the vibration of that passionate energy. A passionate person is one who is *alive*, enthusiastic, and totally present in their love for what they do. You can also see the lack of that passion, and therefore the lack of that life force, in people who are depressed.

For too long, our societies have clothed our sexuality and sensuality in garments of guilt, inhibiting that fabulous energy by wrapping it in a shawl of misplaced righteousness. If we take a look at the world in which we exist, we find that most species on this planet [birds, animals, insects, fish, reptiles, plants] need male and female sexual encounters in some form for them to reproduce and breathe life onto Mother Earth. I believe we would not have been given such energy if it was not also part of the spiritual experience. I also believe there was a great deal of passion around when this amazing cosmos was created.

If you are a creative person, an artist of any kind, and you are not putting into your activity the passion that comes from deep within you, the fire in your belly, your sexual energy, then it is highly likely that your activity will fall short of its potential; the song and dance will be lifeless, the painting will be flat, the writing will be stale.

Everywhere I look I see the energy of divine passion;

- The moon
- Starlight in a velvet-black sky
- The colours of a sunset or sunrise
- The sound of the sea
- The colours of birds and flowers
- The passion in a waterfall
- The grace and beauty of a magnificent tree
- The natural movements of a child at play
- The sparkling eyes of a lover
- The gentle smile on the wise elder

There is no separation between spiritual and sexual energy. They are one of the same. Surely there are few spiritual experiences to compare with the divine beauty of passion that is shared between two loving people involved in a sexual encounter. Like all aspects of our life, such beauty can be abused, but true passion is part of the essence of our soul. Passion, for whatever reason, makes your heart sing.

Have you lost the fire in your belly? You need to take a look at the things you like to do and allow yourself to arouse the passion within your mind, heart, and soul. Then you can enter into your activities with enthusiasm and lightness of heart. It is rejuvenating to explore something new, something different to help bring back passion into your life. Without passion, we only exist, we are not truly living.

I am passionate about the writing of this book. I am passionate about my work as a grief counsellor and a medium. I am passionate about bringing native wild birds back into my garden. And, in these my latter years, I will once again experience that other kind of passion when my lovely ones in spirit bring my new lover to me. I am grateful for this wonderful life that allows me to explore *all* of it with that passion that burns like a fire in my belly.

As I was moving through the grief of my husband's death, I made a choice not just to exist. I made the choice to live, fully and passionately, to heal the wounds, and to explore my new life with fire in my belly. It is now my life-purpose, my joy to help other's ignite their passion and rediscover their beautiful self.

29 *The Power Of The Mind*

I AM BECOMING ACUTELY aware of the power of the mind:

- To destroy or to heal
- To diminish or to raise a person up
- To create a life of drudgery or one of excitement and fulfilment
- To send us into the depths of hell or to raise us up into the heights of heaven

Because we live with our mind every day, we tend to take it for granted and not see how it is powerfully affecting our attitudes, our emotions, our weaknesses, and our strengths.

For many decades, learned authors from many backgrounds of brain therapy have written about the power of the mind, but do we listen? Are we ready to embrace the positive power of the mind? Perhaps the first modern book that really hit the world market, written in layman terms so we could all understand, was Norman Vincent Peale's book *The Power Of Positive Thinking*. Norman's book put those words out into our consciousness to bring us into an awareness of the power of our thoughts. Eckhart Tolle's books, *The Power of Now* and *A New Earth*, are perhaps some of the most powerful books in our present day on the subject of positive thinking. I have recommended

A New Earth to many of my clients because it has so many moments of wonderful wisdom in it.

Psychiatrists, psychologists, scientists, philosophers, and counsellors have been trying to understand the workings of the mind for centuries. This grey matter, housed within our skulls, is one of the greatest miracles that has been created. When it comes to understanding our mind, it is also one of the most elusive to comprehend.

When someone tells me about a person who has a high IQ, my response is to ask, "How are they using it?" I have known people with high IQ's who have been afraid to take up the challenge of exploring their gift of high intelligence. They have drifted through life in a very ordinary way, and that is their right. I have also known people with a relatively low IQ who have achieved greatness through determination and the desire to succeed. Potential remains potential until the person with that potential wants to do something with it. Potential needs action and motivation for it to become a meaningful experience.

I speak with other counsellors, and we agree that the more we explore the miracle of the mind, the more we learn about it the more we understand how little we know. The physical can be explained by science, but the actual thought process and how deeply it impacts upon our lives: will we ever solve that? Are we meant to solve it? Solving how thought works may rob us of the wonder, the delightful mystery of how amazing our brain is.

We take so much for granted without questioning this miracle of a mind within a brain. Where does insight come from? How do we gather wisdom? How does this storage bank in our brain work? How does the brain keep on working while we are fast asleep, creating dreams and visions? How can a medium, such as me, see the past, present and future of another human being? And how can

I see into the realm of spirit and communicate with those who are not in human form? And how do those in spirit, who do not have a physical brain, converse with me? I don't have all the answers, and I am constantly in awe of my connection to spirit and how it all works.

Then there is free will, which allows the mind to be in a place of negative thought or positive thought. Powerful as the mind is, our free will has the greater power. We are the ones in control of our minds. We can allow the negative thoughts to bring us down, diminish us, sabotage everything we do, and create a hellish existence. Or we have the free will to steer our mind towards positive thought, towards achievement, success, and happiness.

After my Jeff died, I realised that some people believed that he was the strong one in our marriage. They approached me with so much helpful advice that I felt swamped by their desire to see me take certain steps and live in a certain way. I had to close off the wishes of other people, to take time out from the world. I had to realise I had the free will to allow others to manipulate my mind [and therefore my life], or I had the free will to be an individual thinker, sorting out what was right for me.

A positive mind is one that also brings us into a deeper understanding of who we are, researching how we can become greater than who we are right now. A positive mind allows us to forgive ourselves and another, letting go of the pain and stepping into the healing. It reaches for the heights of happiness and the depths of peace. A positive mind not only gains knowledge but also gathers wisdom and sees that all experiences, negative and positive, are opportunities to learn more of who we are.

The more positive are our thoughts, the stronger is our link with those who are working with us in spirit. Our loved ones in spirit and our spirit guides love a strong, individual, and positive mind.

Our lives begin to flow in a stream of abundance in all of its forms, because we are not pushing upstream against the direction our soul wants to go: toward happiness.

A positive mind + positive action = a fulfilled and happy life.

30 *Leaving This World*

YOU MAY HAVE HEARD the saying: a person comes into this world with nothing on his back and leaves this world with nothing on his back! And I say not so.

Of course the saying refers to material possessions, and in that respect it is right. So enjoy the possessions you have to the fullest, without allowing yourself to become a slave to those possessions. When those possessions become our master, they can destroy the joyfulness in our life.

I don't believe we leave this world with nothing on our backs. I believe we either leave with a heavy burden, or we leave knowing that what we carry into our next life is a great deal of wisdom.

Where do we want to be when we are dying? Do we want to leave feeling that our life has been disastrous or that we have completed what we came here to do?

Ah yes, I hear the question: what did I come into this life to do? Some of us know the answer and are walking our chosen path; some of us know the answer but, through fear, are avoiding that path; and some of us will still be searching for the path. For those who are still searching, enjoy the treasure hunt! Perhaps your chosen path is not in the doing but in the discovery of who you are.

Each lifetime, we choose the challenges we need to face:

- For the expansion and growth of our soul
- For the gathering of wisdom and knowledge
- To have the opportunity to overcome our fears
- To have the chance to cleanse and heal the traumas of past lives and this life

Ultimately, we are all on this planet to learn one single lesson: *how to live a happy and joyful life*. It is the accomplishment of this lesson that we need to carry with us through the curtain of death, to enter the realm of spirit with a joyful heart and a glowing soul.

Happiness! How does one obtain happiness? Happiness is the end product of love, self-love. It seems to me that happiness has three levels: imagined happiness, happiness through an event, or real happiness that is an inner journey.

- Imagined happiness: If only I could do this, have that, pay those bills, get that job I would be happy. If only!
- Happiness through the outcome of an event: I am so happy because I have got a new lover, new job, a world trip to go on, or a rise in my salary. This kind of happiness is short-lived because it is reliant upon something or someone outside of us creating that happiness for us.
- Real happiness: A happiness that is found within us that is a fountain of joy always present, always waiting for us to discover it. A happiness that comes from learning to accept and love self. A happiness that comes from knowing that we were born perfect and that, in our inner most being, our soul-self, we still are perfect. When we find our divinity to balance our humanity, then we find that fountain of joy!

With joyfulness comes peace and contentment. Not the peace that comes with quiet surroundings and lack of quarrels. The peace I am referring to is the inner peace where fear cannot abide, the inner peace of stillness that is present in the midst of the outer turmoil of life. As a nurse, I could physically see the difference between those who died having this inner peace and those who died carrying a heavy burden. That which remains unresolved in this lifetime will be waiting for us to resolve in another lifetime.

We are not alone in our life. Our loved ones in spirit walk with us. Our guides in spirit walk with us. It is hard at times for us to comprehend what that looks like and how it works. We are trapped in a physical body that makes it difficult for most of us to understand the realm of spirit. But that does not negate the presence of those beautiful beings. They are ever so patient and loving. I know from my own experience that my loved ones, who walk with me in spirit, have had a tough time of it with this student of the soul.

We and only we are the masters of our lives. Those in spirit are there to help us. They cannot and will not interfere with the decisions we make. We have a thing called free will, and our guides and loved ones honour our right to exercise that free will. As much as we might like to blame them or others for what is happening in our lives, we are the only creators of our lives. We choose to be happy or miserable. We choose to be lazy or over-worked. We choose to be relaxed or tense. We choose to stay in a destructive relationship or to get out of it. We choose to stand in the light or sit in darkness. And.....

We choose to walk with spirit.....or not!

Journey well, my fellow travellers!

REFERENCE BOOKS

Brian Weiss

- *Many Lives, Many Masters* ISBN: 13 978-0-671-65786-4 Fireside (Simon and Schuster). The true story of a prominent psychiatrist, his young patient, and the past-life therapy that changed both their lives.
- *Messages From The Masters* ISBN: 0 7499-2167-6 Piatkus Books Limited. Tapping into the power of love.

Eckart Tolle

- *A New Earth* ISBN: 978-0-7181-4857-7 Penguin. Awakening to your life's purpose.
- *The Power of Now* ISBN: 0-7336-1376-4 Hodder. A guide to spiritual enlightenment.

Dr Michael Newton

- *Journey of Souls* ISBN: 978-1-56718-485-3 Llewellyn Publications. Case studies of life between lives.
- *Destiny of Souls* ISBN: 13: 978-1-56718-499-0 Llewellyn Publications. New case studies of life between lives.

John Holland

- *The Spirit Whisperer* ISBN: 978-1-4019-2287-0 Hay House. Chronicles of a medium.
- *Born knowing* Hay House. John's story of accepting and developing his abilities as a medium.

Gordon Smith

- *The Unbelievable Truth* ISBN: 1-4019-0603-6 Hay House. A medium's insider guide to the unseen world.
- *Life Changing Messages* ISBN: 978-1-4019-1567-4 Hay House. Remarkable stories from the other side.

Gary Zukav

- *The Seat of The Soul* Free Press (New York Times No. 1 Bestseller) The purpose of the soul and where it resides within us.
- *Soul to Soul* ISBN: 13 978-1-4165-6467-6 Free Press. Communications from the heart.

Norman Vincent Peale

- *The Power of Positive Thinking* Using the power of the mind to create a happy and productive life.

Doreen Virtue

- See Doreen's website www.angeltherapy.com for information on Doreen's courses and her books.

Denise Linn

- *The Hidden Power Of Dreams* ISBN: 978-1-4019-1791-3 Hay House. The mysterious world of dreams revealed.

Kahlil Gibran

- *The Prophet* ISBN: 978-1-78028-435-4 Lifetime. Timeless wisdom.

Dr Steven Farmer

- *Animal Spirit Guides* ISBN: 13 978-1-4019-0733-4 Hay House. Handbook for identifying and understanding your power animals and animal spirit helpers.

Dr. John F Demartini

- *The Breakthrough Experience* ISBN: 13 978-1-56170-885-7 Hay House. A revolutionary new approach to personal transformation.

Dr Melvin Morse

- *Parting Visions* ISBN 0-679-42754-6 Villard Books. Uses and meanings of pre-death, psychic, and spiritual experiences.

Dr Robert Holden

- *Be Happy* ISBN: 978-1-4019-2181-1 Hay House. Release the power of happiness in you.

Joy Brisbane

- *When Do The Tears Stop*? ISBN: 978-1-4520-6403-1 Author House. Through grief's night into a new day.
- *Spirit Speaks* ISBN: 978-1-5043-0390-3 Balboa Press

Theta Energy Healing

- *Go Up And Seek God* ISBN: 0-9671754-0-2 Rolling Thunder. 12 strand DNA technique for healing and enlightenment.
- *Go Up And Work With God* ISBN: 0-9671754-1-0 Rolling Thunder. An alternative healing technique.
- www.thetahealing.com

Patch Adams

- See DVD Patch Adams www.patchadams.org The story of an amazing doctor who saw the power of using humour to help the process of healing.

Printed in the United States
By Bookmasters